AF394159

Beyond Belief

Beyond Belief

Theoaesthetics or Just Old-Time Religion?

Edited by

RONALD R. BERNIER

PICKWICK *Publications* · Eugene, Oregon

Pickwick Publications
An Imprint of Wipf and Stock Publishers
199 W. 8th Ave., Suite 3
Eugene, OR 97401

www.wipfandstock.com

ISBN 13: 978-1-60899-087-0

Cataloging-in-Publication data:

Beyond belief : theoaesthetics or just old-time religion? / edited by
Ronald R. Bernier.

viii + 142 p.; 23 cm.

ISBN 13: 978-1-60899-087-0

1. Aesthetics — Religious aspects. 2. Christianity and the arts. 3. Art and
Religion. 4. Art and society. I. Bernier, Ronald R. II. Title.

BR115 A8 B55 2010

Manufactured in the U.S.A.

Contents

Illustrations

Introduction

RONALD R. BERNIER

Once upon a time—but really, in every place,
and in every time—art was religious.[1]

THE MUTUAL ESTRANGEMENT OF art and religion is the proud legacy of modernity. There was a time, however, as James Elkins reminds us, when the aesthetic and the spiritual were of a piece.

This collection of essays explores the possible re-emergence of a theological dimension to contemporary art, called by some a *re-enchantment* of art. "Re-enchantment, as I understand it," writes Suzi Gablik, "means stepping beyond the modern traditions of mechanism, positivism, empiricism, rationalism, materialism, secularism, and scientism—the whole objectifying consciousness of the Enlightenment—in a way that allows for a return of the soul."[2] Long estranged from symbol and sacrament, artists seem to have turned once again to a vision rooted in the soul, where "soul" may be taken to mean something like Hegel's all-embracing "Spirit," that which transcends isolated individuality and joins us with other people and communities—art as a way of re-humanizing us. Soul, or spirit, in this sense, is ultimately so-

---

1. James Elkins, *On the Strange Place of Religion in Contemporary Art* (London: Routledge, 2004).

2. Suzi Gablik, *The Re-Enchantment of Art* (New York: Thames & Hudson, 1991) 11.

"

cial, one's sense of participation and membership—however real or imagined—in a shared totality or humanity. In an era marked culturally by world-weary cynicism and self-conscious irony, a new humanism may be emerging both in art practice and, hopefully, in its critical discourses.

Thierry De Duve, who has argued instead for a continued faith in the Enlightenment paradigm that others have generally agreed has failed us, and whose clear desire is that artists *not* engage lingering interests in spirituality, still finds it necessary to argue that "The best modern art has endeavored to redefine the essentially *religious* terms of humanism on *belief-less* bases."[3] "Belief" here is arguably understood as the modern notion of intellectual assent, with onto-theological implications—absent, I suggest, from an understanding of belief as faith and faith as trust. Indeed, "beyond belief" in dogma, to faith as the substance of things hoped for. Postmodern thinker Marc C. Taylor, goes much further, and identifies a *theoesthetic* "in which art and religion join to lead individuals and society from fragmentation and opposition to integration and unification."[4] Clearly the matter is not resolved. "Art and faith," arbitrates William Dyrness, "both strain at the boundaries in which they are placed. They slip out of our grasp because they both deal in wonder. Maybe our conversation ought at least to remember this fact, and acknowledge that both are, ultimately, not within our control. That would be a start. All sides, it would seem, have much to gain from such humility."[5] Important point, and we do well to concede it here.

The aim of these essays is not to propose a resurgence of religious iconography, but rather to give voice to long-suppressed— often maligned, and certainly professionally risky—positions

3. Thierry de Duve, *Look: 100 Years of Contemporary Art* (Ghent: Ludion, 2001) 14.

4. Marc C. Taylor, *Disfiguring: Art, Architecture and Religion* (Chicago: University of Chicago Press, 1992) 46.

5. James Elkins and David Morgan, eds., *Re-Enchantment* (New York: Rutledge, 2009) 229.

informed by and reverberating with themes of the sacred. Indeed in the introduction to his much-quoted 2004 book, *On the Strange Place of Religion in Contemporary Art,* James Elkins succinctly describes my own sense of disquiet in proposing the theme of this gathering, originally a session at the 2008 annual conference of the College Art Association: "For people in my profession of art history," Elkins writes, "the very fact that I have written this book may be enough to cast me into a dubious category of fallen and marginal historians who somehow don't get modernism or postmodernism."[6] This is, the critic is arguing, a general tendency within the art world to see art that invokes religion in any but a critical way as retrograde and reactionary. That is to say, religion today is seldom treated in the art and academic worlds unless it is coupled with recrimination, ironic distance, or scandal. "[T]he absence of openly religious art from modern art museums," further contends Elkins, "would seem to be due to the prejudices of a coterie of academic writers who have become unable to acknowledge what has always been apparent: art and religion are entwined."[7]

The present contribution to the debate, however, aims to challenge the assumed secularism of institutional art history and the pervasive skepticism when it comes to religion as a topic of discussion in the academy. The question I posed to the scholars included here was, again drawing from Elkins, whether it is achievable "to adjust the existing discourse enough to make it possible to address both secular theorists and religionists who would normally consider themselves outside the artworld."[8] And, I would add, beyond our contemporary—and thoroughly unhelpful—model of the secular left and the evangelical right. What these very different essays share is a commitment to that discourse, a coming to terms with faith as part of the fabric of the social, and, more specifically, speculating on the place of the

---

6. Elkins, *On the Strange Place of Religion,* xi.

7. Ibid., ix.

8. Ibid., xi.

sacred in contemporary visual culture. Collectively, the authors approach these issues from a number of different and diverging perspectives, ranging from classroom pedagogy and curatorial practice, to theoretical speculation on theological aesthetics, to contemporary art-making in painting, sculpture, installation, film and performance. And while diverse in their observations and conclusions, one thing that became strikingly clear in bringing them together, first in the conference session and then here in this collection of papers, is that religious awareness, as Marc C. Taylor has argued, "slips away in the very effort to grasp it, the unity it portends can only be 'present' as 'absent.'" This dialectic in art—of disclosure and concealment, presence and absence, or meaning as the promise of presence through embodied absence, neither fully here and now nor entirely elsewhere and beyond— is what makes this topic so engaging and indeed so timely.

A word about structure and arrangement. As convener of the original CAA session and as compiler of the revised essays here, I have assumed an editor's privilege in positioning the essays in such a way that, although not part of their original presentation, forms a dialogic exchange—a theoretical argument is "answered" or "responded" to or "encountered" or taken up in some other way by an essay on artistic practice, in a sense theology "done" through the use of, or by appeal to, actual physical artistic media. And this for a reason: in the time spent reading, reviewing and reflecting on the various positions offered here, there emerged just such a kind of dialogue between certain essays that, I felt, would be illuminating for readers.

Finally, what is offered here is, admittedly, a deliberately un-integrated conversation—perhaps many conversational threads; readers looking for resolution or consensus will be disappointed. But this speaks, I think, to the complexity and density of the issues addressed—art and religion, art and faith in a postmodern world. Its purpose is to invite more voices into this noisy debate, and to prompt more of something we might call "theoaesthetic thinking."

Chapters one and three, by Daniel Siedell and Jason Danner respectively, take wide-ranging philosophical perspectives to set our foundation for a possible theological aesthetics. Siedell's opening essay, "Liturgical Aesthetics and Contemporary Artistic Practice," begins with the claim that the contemporary art world, in its *practice*, has of late grown increasingly uncomfortable with its inherited condition of "unbelief." He argues for contemporary artistic practices that, despite an intolerant *critical* culture, actively undermine a moribund Enlightenment opposition between institutional "religion" and individual "spirituality," by appropriating one of religion's most important—but, he contends, overlooked—characteristics: its sacramental and liturgical identity. He argues that religion is an embodied public practice that assumes that the divine comes to us through matter, through ordinary and mundane material practices such as rituals, behaviors, and spaces that are imbued with sacred meaning. Siedell considers a liturgical framework, anchored within the ancient Christian tradition of ecumenical councils, to throw into relief the connections between religion, art, and ethics as social practices that some contemporary art can—and does—embody, and, as the following essay shows, often in approaches that are less object-centered than practice-centered, allowing the sacred to be considered as a social process. Liturgy (belief or faith), in other words, as *performed*.

In chapter two, Karen Gonzalez Rice, takes up this question of the relationship between aesthetic and ascetic practice by exploring the performance art of former Maryknoll novice, Linda Montano, within the context of ritual and rule- or "vow"-based monastic discipline and the discipleship of "formation." She closely considers *Art/Life: One Year Performance* (1983–1984), in which Montano remained tied to performance artist Tehching Tseih by an eight-foot rope for one year, and the longer-term piece *Seven Years of Living Art* (1984–1991), in which the artist took on a different persona each year, and where strict guidelines dictated everything from the color of Montano's clothing to the frequency and type of physical contact with others, and even the tenor of her thoughts. In the form of the "vow," individual discipline is linked with collaborative engagement in monastic life. Gonzalez Rice argues here that in Montano's performances, the artist negotiates the inevitable *tensions* between self and community, isolation and encounter, making visible a mapping of the bodily practices of monasticism onto her performance—and, in a real sense, sacramental—actions. Liturgy as a species of performance.

Then, in chapter three, "Theology and Art in the Postmodern Desert," Jason A. Danner,[9] considers the work of the Cambridge school of Radical Orthodoxy, and in particular the work of post-secular theologians John Milbank, Graham Ward, Catherine Pickstock, Philip Blond, and others, philosophers committed to the project of "restoring the vital artery" of aesthetics to theology, and this as a rejoinder to a Kantian aesthetics of the sublime. These contemporary theologians, Danner argues, propose centering aesthetics on a revelatory experience of God's transcendence, too transcendent to be subdued or tamed, as Kant had it, by the mitigating offices of human reason. Such a revelation, Danner concludes, leaves one radically transformed, one's subjectivity irrevocably altered, the self "unselfed." And to do this he invokes Radical Orthodoxy's critique of aesthetic modes of retreat from the revelation of transcendence and the Kantian—and Enlightenment—aggrandizement of the modern subject. While these approaches do not offer an explicit aesthetics of the epiphanic encounter, Danner allows, neither do they foreclose the possibility; in fact, they invite it.

Indeed, it is that invitation, couched in a defense of the Kantian sublime, that I take up in chapter four in my essay, "*In*

---

9. While Danner's paper was originally included for presentation at the CAA conference, he was unfortunately unable to present it; it is included here because it offered an important contribution to the original session as envisioned.

Excess: Jean-Luc Marion, Bill Viola and the Theological Sublime."[10] The Kantian sublime, I argue, was that experience that reveals to mind Nature's power to intimate what is visually unrepresentable. In the presence of the Sublime we are reminded that Nature as manifold is not ours to know completely; our perceptual faculties, rendered incapacitated by the sheer immensity of that plenitude, are overwhelmed, resulting in an estimation of power which relocates the self into an awareness of one's own limited position in a limitless universe. In its reemergence in the postmodern world, I suggest, this very experience of disproportion between the mind's ordering power and an ungraspable complexity, serves as an *analogue* of something else—the infinite, the divine—and thus the consolation that something transcends our ordinary and finite phenomenal being. Using the high-tech apparatus of modern video, American artist Bill Viola's art is, I propose, rooted precisely in this theological tradition of transcendent experience. The technological apparatus of modern image making—high speed film, high definition video, LCD and plasma screens, and sophisticated sound recording—are put to use by Viola in ways that significantly challenge prevailing intellectual and artistic traditions and return art to the power of the Sublime—and to an aesthetic of *revelation*.

In chapter five, "The Pursuit of Beauty vs. The Aesthetics of Worldmakers," Arthur Pontynen vigorously argues in a different theoretical direction, in fact taking issue with the central question of this project, and that is the possibility of a "theo-aesthetic humanism." His argument begins with the basic and shared claim that modernism is associated with the Enlightenment, and that the Enlightenment alleges that we should escape from superstition, ignorance, and religion via the pursuit of a scientific rationality. This modernist denial of *why*, as he calls it, the denial of meaning and purpose, is a denial of virtually all the fine art produced

---

10. This paper was not presented in the 2008 CAA conference. Rather, it is a revised version of a paper presented at the 2009 annual conference of the Association of Art Historians in Manchester, UK.

before the Modernist era. Furthermore, Pontynen contends, it marks a reduction of culture from the pursuit of beauty to *mere* aesthetics—art relegated, as he sees it, to entertainment, therapy, or propaganda.[11] Borrowing the concept of "worldmaking" from Nelson Goodman, Pontynen posits that as worldmakers, religion is not denied, but immanentized. We are, he suggests, both the creators and destroyers of our worlds and the worlds of others. The primary advocates of the Modernist tradition—Kant, Hegel, Sartre, Heidegger, among others—all advocate that humanity play the role of god. Thus, lurking behind the mask of Modernist rationality, according to Pontynen, is not so much secularism as willful self-deification. It is, then, he counters, beauty as the splendor of truth and goodness that Modernism seeks to destroy. As such it trivializes and brutalizes reason, culture, and humanity. The solution, he suggests, is finally to escape the dogmatism not of religion, but of the Modernist paradigm, and the restoration of the much maligned notions of Truth, Goodness, and Beauty.[12]

The following chapter, "A Secular Trinity? The Transformation of Christian Iconography in a Post-Christian Age," challenges such orthodoxy. Here Michelle Lang considers the dissonance within dogmatic, mainstream Christianity, and its refusal to embrace postmodern relativism, and which, moreover, sees the arts as ontologically suspect and morally threatening. Lang argues that a theological aesthetics, which she sees as approaching the problem of the relationship between art and the divine from the exclusive perspective of traditional Christian doctrine, as relevant only to believers, as it demands a suspension of critical methods not grounded in Scripture or exegesis. It is Lang's position that the discipline of art history—at least as presently configured and practiced—is comfortable only with exploring religious iconography and an interpretive context where the subject in question

---

11. This is decidedly different from Siedell's and Danner's (and my) notion of the aesthetic as theology.

12. And in this, I think, Pontynen shares more ground with Siedell and Danner (and me) than on first hearing might be acknowledged.

is safely removed from the present. Yet, she maintains, art continues to express that most fundamental of human concerns—our relationship to the numinous—and artists use various strategies to achieve this, particularly artists who approach the representation of "God" through what can be theologically understood as a secularized version of the Christian Trinity. She thoughtfully explores what would constitute an alternative representation of the divine and how this would affect Christology and the doctrine of the Trinity. Specifically Lang invokes Process Theology (and "postmodern green theology"), which moves away from common deistic, monarchical, and agential theories of the relationship between God and the world to posit a more organic model where the divine is both transcendent and immanent. As evidence of such, Lang offers the work of Canadian artists Emily Carr and Mary Pratt, to consider a loosening of the traditional iconography of Christianity while still creating a space for the spiritual content of art without being confined by its dogma and its absolutes. The work of these artists, as well as others like Andy Goldsworthy and Christo, Lang contends, provide a relevant framework for allusions to the numinous that engage postmodern concerns with science, the environment, the body, and technologies of the visual.

Finally, the collaborative effort from Scott Parsons and David O'Hara, "Visual Culture and the Sacred: Creative Acts of Resistance and Redemption in Art, Film, and New Media," calls upon many of the issues raised throughout this book by bringing them into the classroom and reflecting on their own experience as educators—O'Hara in philosophy and Parsons a studio arts professor and public artist—teaching a course in contemporary art, religion, and visual culture. In this fascinating "report from the field"—how art is taught and judged—O'Hara and Parsons ask graduating seniors in their final semester at Augustana College in Sioux Falls, South Dakota, to reflect in an ethical way on the whole of their liberal arts education and subsequently to ask: "How then shall we live?" (A rare question indeed, especially in departments of art history.) The results are fascinating and their report maps the trajectory of a course—from its conceptualization to its outcomes—that combines history, theory, and practice in a way that gets non-art majors engaged in producing and thinking about the role of art in their pursuit of what matters most in their lives, and people from diverse religious traditions engaged in a conversation about the numinous and the transcendent apart from dogma.

Thus we are returned to the question with which we began, prompted as it was by James Elkins's modest but rich examination of "the strange place of religion in contemporary art:" Is it possible thinking past the mutual mistrust of art and religion, to re-read and re-engage spiritual themes within postmodern culture? The scholars gathered here propose—and contest—an alternative perspective on the "human condition," one that speculates on the place of the numinous and the life of faith in contemporary art, and opens up the field of inquiry to include appreciation of affective nuances of lived encounter. In effect, the goal here has been to test the adequacy of visual culture to lived human experience and to the deeply felt life, and in so doing to consider the key features of any contemporary theological aesthetics—that it be revelatory, participatory, and transformative. And as we began, so we shall close, with James Elkins's eloquent reminder that we must continue to reflect on the relation between visual culture and the sacred: "It is impossible to talk sensibly about religion and at the same time address art in an informed and intelligent manner: but it is also irresponsible not to keep trying."[13]

13. Elkins, *On the Strange Place of Religion*, 116.

1

Liturgical Aesthetics and Contemporary Artistic Practice

Some Remarks on Developing a Critical Framework

Daniel A. Siedell

There is more reason in your body than in your best Wisdom.
—Friedrich Nietzsche, *Thus Spoke Zarathustra*

They [the gods] string us together on a threat of song and dance. . . .
—Plato, *Laws*

I

MODERNITY FREED ART FROM service to religion, or so critics and art historians have strongly asserted. But religion did not nor will it go away. It haunts modern art because both religion and art require belief for them to work. For example, just as for the Eucharist to be efficacious, the recipient must believe (i.e., have faith) that the wine and wafer is the blood and body of Christ, so too must the beholder of a work of art believe that the oil paint smeared on a canvas surface means something.[1] In various ways and in various degrees, artists have sensed this kinship between artistic and religious practice. But critics and art historians have sought simply to deny this presence. Their stubborn assertions of autonomy amount to nothing more than whistling in the dark and the denial that art, religion, philosophy, and science are kinfolk, are each different but related manifestations of what Irish philosopher William Desmond calls, "being mindful of what is it to be."[2] In a recent symposium on "re-enchantment and art" organized and moderated by art historian James Elkins at the School of the Art Institute of Chicago, critic Thierry de Duve suggested that the secular (anti-religious) project of the Enlightenment be given more time.[3] It is only three centuries old, he reminds us. De Duve's comment is reminiscent of G. K. Chesterton's assertion that Christianity has not failed; but that it has not yet been tried. Such Panglossian optimism in the Enlightenment secular project, which appears now to be just another form of blind religious faith that does not realize its nature as faith, underwrites modernist art criticism, which proceeds only by heroic acts of reduction, chopping down both art and religion to fit the Procrustean Bed of Enlightenment secularism. But both art and religion have been stubborn victims, often refusing to submit to such violence by defying the strict parameters imposed by modernist critics, namely, that art is a critical and self-reflective aesthetic exploration of form (or an index of signs) while religious belief is uncritical and unreflective, transferred through habit and tradition, and thus without rational foundation.

Like religious fundamentalists, modernist art critics justify their faith and practice by relying upon the most simplistic and

---

1. For a fuller exploration of this theme, see my "Enrique Martinez Celaya's *Thing and Deception* (1997): The Aesthetic Practice of Belief," *Religion and the Arts* 10/1 (2006).

2. William Desmond, *Art, Origins, Otherness: Between Philosophy and Art* (Albany: SUNY Press, 2003) 29. 4.

3. See "Art Seminar," in James Elkins and David Morgan, eds., *Re-enchantment* (London: Routledge, 2008) 114–15.

clichéd caricature of their opponent without the least bit of self-reflection on their part as to the belief their work requires. For the modernist art critics, this means that they continue to sneer at a portrait of religion hastily and crudely drawn by philosophers three centuries ago and snort at contemporary religious believers as somewhat sub-rational.[4] This portrait regards religion to be a public embodiment of collective belief, mediated through history, tradition, and dogma that limits independent thought, stifles creativity, and is unable to stand up to the Enlightenment standards of autonomous reason. Moreover, the secular rationalists claim that religion is disappearing from the modern world. In response to one such manifestation of this attitude Eastern Orthodox theologian and cultural polemicist David Bentley Hart makes this pungent observation:

> Surely, I thought as I was reading, this is a man in whom parochialism has metastasized into a psychosis. Here we are living in an age when Christianity is spreading more rapidly and more widely than at any other point in the two millennia of its history—throughout the global South and East—and yet, because the Church languishes in the senile cultures of a small geological apophysis (with a few appertinent isles) at the western edge of continental Asia, [A. N.] Wilson concludes that the faith is in its death throes.[5]

The "senile cultures of a small geological apophysis," to which Hart refers in this excoriation, are those intellectuals of the Western European Enlightenment, who project their own secularist aspirations on the "modern world." But they remain aspirations, aspirations that, ironically, require a kind of religious belief or faith to maintain. And so, not surprisingly, religion remains the generative and creative force for most work, even irreligious or anti-religious work. Furthermore, the world is not becoming

4. See, for example, the journalistic work of the atheist fundamentalists Christopher Hitchins and Richard Dawkins.

5. David Bentley Hart, "Beyond Disbelief," *New Criterion* 23/10 (2005).

more secular as society becomes more modern, as the sociologists told us it would. In fact, Peter Berger, who was one of those sociologists that shaped the so-called "secularization theory," has recently recanted.[6] (The forms that such religious and spiritual practices are now taking have shifted, but that is another issue.) Enlightenment rationality emerged out of, not merely in reaction to, the Protestant Reformation in the sixteenth century, which affirmed a radical individualism, freedom of conscience, suspicion of "empty" tradition and "dead" ritual. In fact, the very notions of a secular sphere and inward experience were Protestant inventions. Kant's, Hegel's, and Nietzsche's philosophical projects are inconceivable without their pietistic Lutheran tradition.[7] Henri de Saint-Simon, the French Utopian Socialist who appropriated the term "avant-garde" in 1824 that provided the ideological underpinnings that have sustained artists to the present, called the artist and the intellectual the new "priest class" in a modern, secularized and scientifically-based society. Moreover, Saint-Simon wrote an essay called "The New Christianity" only a year later, in which he commends none other than Martin Luther.[8] The Enlightenment project, in which Saint Simon's reflections on a "new" Christianity participate, has sought to break through the calcified crust of organized religion to penetrate into the deeper, richer, hotter, and more powerful, yet hidden realm, where "authentic" reason and "authentic" spirituality dwell. Everywhere an enlightened rationalist looks, religion lurks. However, the Enlightenment project, following the iconoclasm of the Protestant Reformers' mantra,

6. See Peter Berger, ed., *The Desecularization of the World: Resurgent Religion and World Politics* (Grand Rapids: Eerdmans, 1999).

7. See Cyril O'Regan, *Heterodox Hegel* (Albany: SUNY Press, 1994); Bruce Ellis Benson, *Pious Nietzsche: Decadence and Dionysian Faith* (Bloomington: Indiana University Press, 2008); and C. Firstone and S. Palmquist, eds., *Kant and the New Philosophy of Religion* (Bloomington: Indiana University Press, 2006).

8. See Henri de Saint-Simon, "The New Christianity: First Dialogue" (1825), in Keith Taylor, ed. and trans. *Henri de Saint-Simon: Selected Writings on Science, Industry, and Social Organization* (London: Croom Helm, 1975) 289–304.

semper reformanda ("always reforming"), sowed the seeds for undermining its own self-asserting authority through the postmodern critique of certain aspects of rationality—in the very service of the Enlightenment ideals. And so Postmodern thought has engendered what has been called the "religious" turn in Continental theory, as such thinkers as Lyotard, Levinas, Jean-Luc Marion, Derrida, Bataille, Slavoj Zizek, Jean-Luc Nancy, John Caputo, William Desmond, and others have initiated a more nuanced philosophical reflection on and through religion. In fact, historian Bruce Holsinger convincingly argues that the emergence of postmodern theory, from Georges Bataille and Roland Barthes, to Derrida and Foucault, is predicated on a rediscovery and creative appropriation of the intellectual energy of the Middle Ages.[9] However, as Holsinger demonstrates, the thinkers themselves (and especially their disciples) were less than forthcoming about their debts.

The recent interest in the contemporary art world in things spiritual, exemplified in numerous exhibitions on the subject, might suggest a defiance of the intellectual framework of the Enlightenment that are part of a "religious" turn in contemporary art criticism. But this is not the case. Despite the importance of a renewed and revitalized interest in the relationship between art and spirituality, criticism remains defined by Enlightenment categories. Unfortunately, as James Elkins has rightly observed, the religious turn in Continental philosophy, with its more richly textured and expansive understanding of religion and its relationship to art and philosophy, has yet to make a serious impact on the discourse on contemporary art.[10] Art critics continue to invoke Continental theory as if it had no interest in religion whatsoever. (But, like playing with Ouija boards, one cannot play with serious thinkers without risking the invocation of unwanted

9. Bruce Holsinger, *The Premodern Condition: Medievalism and the Making of Theory* (Chicago: University of Chicago Press, 2005).

10. James Elkins, *On the Strange Place of Religion in Contemporary Art* (London: Routledge, 2005).

religious ghosts.) Contemporary art discourse thus remains defined by an Enlightenment-based framework that pits matter against the spiritual, the immanent against the transcendent, and the spiritual against the religious. Therefore, critical discourse fumbles and flails along in this prison house of Enlightenment rationalism, either producing anorexic art criticism, obsessed with its own distorted reflection of Byzantine sophistication and depth, as it follows the letter and ignores the robust spirit of Continental thought, or producing bloated and gossipy journalism that trades in the "star power" of the contemporary art world. However, contemporary artistic practice gladly undermines such Manichean oppositions, and their practice affirms the fact that art and religion come from the same source, that place between the univocal and the equivocal, between immanence and transcendence, between being and becoming. A closer examination of religion is required in order to properly understand the implications of some contemporary artistic practice that works between the boundaries of art, philosophy, science, and religion. In so doing, we might come to appreciate more fully the wisdom of Wittgenstein's enigmatic observation and its relevance for many artists: "I am not a religious man but I cannot help seeing everything from a religious point of view."[11]

II

What is a religious point of view? The heart and soul of any religion is its liturgy.

Religion is not merely or simply "believed," as if it is the sum total of our intellectual thoughts about it; it is *practiced*. From the Greek, *leitourgos*, which means literally, "the work of people," liturgy is religion's work. In his seminal essay, "The Trace of the Other" (1963), Levinas suggests that liturgy is "the work of the Self in the sense of a movement, without return to the Self,

---

11. Quoted in Fergus Kerr, *Theology After Wittgenstein* (Oxford: Blackwell, 1986) 33.

toward the Other."[12] Liturgy is the means by which our ethical responsibility—what we owe each other and what we owe to the Divine—is worked out. And in fact, Levinas states, "the liturgy is the ethical." With its cyclical repetitions, structures of blessing and doxology, Levinas sees in liturgical expression a means to approach the Other without dissolving either the Self or the Other. The Other is present, but as a trace, as an "absent presence" or a "present absence," which cannot be absorbed into the Self, which is the urge of the Enlightenment project. The liturgy also reconfigures and revalues time. Liturgy, as theologian Catherine Pickstock suggests, "imagines something in excess of everyday life," an excess that "relativizes the everyday without denying its value."[13] It accumulates the past into a living present, which projects a future—at that moment—that neither denies nor worships the past and the future, but produces a living present moment of expectation, transforming the present into a means for transcendence. Moreover, liturgy practices repetition, a repetition that is, however, never redundant, but always new. This is echoed in Kierkegaard's pithy quip, "repetition is the true eternity."[14] In other words, time, as *Chronos*, that of mundane sequential time, which speaks of death, is embraced, and thus transformed, by *Kairos*, a sacred time "in between," a cyclical return that is, however, never the same, never monotonous, as it incorporates and enfolds mundane events into its movements all the while recapitulating the past. Liturgical practice is thus oriented toward the future while at the same time remembering significant moments in the past. Indeed, these everyday events are given meaning through this dynamic of anticipation and recollection. Space is also trans-

12. Emmanuel Levinas, "The Trace of the Other" (1963), trans. A. Lingis, in *Deconstruction in Context: Literature and Philosophy*, Mark C. Taylor, ed. (Chicago: University of Chicago Press, 1986) 345–59.

13. Catherine Pickstock, "Liturgy, Art, and Politics," *Modern Theology* 16/2 (April 2000) 165, 161. I rely heavily on this essay and Pickstock, *After Writing: On the Liturgical Consummation of Philosophy* (Oxford: Blackwell, 1998).

14. Søren Kierkegaard, *Repetition*, trans. Howard V. Hong and Edna H. Hong (Princeton: Princeton University Press, 1983) 327.

formed in liturgical practice; it is set apart. Both space and time are thus transfigured in and through the liturgy, transformed for ethical work. Through the liturgy, individuality is not denied but affirmed. Such corporate, communal action *produces* the individual. This individual is not the self-assertive, self-contained autonomous Cartesian Cogito, but an ethically responsible individual whose very essence is defined in and through work toward another. Liturgical practice thus assumes a particular comportment toward being that undermines Enlightenment rationality. In fact, as Pickstock argues, liturgical practice exposes modernity to have produced a "pseudo" liturgy or a "parody" of the liturgy, an "antiliturgy liturgy."[15] Liturgical practice embodies Heidegger's notion of the "thrownness" of being; that is, that the source of our being lies outside us. We do not determine our being. Thought always already occurs in the midst of being, grounding such thought. We can only think and act being in the midst of being. Rather than deny this situation, liturgical expression preserves it as a mystery and, significantly, regards it as a gift, not as a curse. Liturgical expression reveals, revels in, and preserves this space "between" Self and Other, between Being and what is beyond Being, in large part through the "middle voice," a voice neither active nor passive, but attentive to what Desmond has called, "the porosity of being." In *Is There a Sabbath for Thought? Between Religion and Philosophy*, Desmond suggests that Sacramental rituals keep open a space of porosity between the human soul and what ultimately exceeds it, even if also in intimate communication with it. This offered a way of dwelling in the world, with a non-literalistic mindfulness, a poetry of the divine.[16]

This porosity is embodied in the liturgy's circumvention of the great Enlightenment dichotomies and autonomies, such as the individual and the community; Self and Other; matter and spirit; immanence and transcendence; even space and

15. Pickstock, "Liturgy, Art, and Politics," 159.

16. William Desmond, *Is There a Sabbath for Thought? Between Religion and Philosophy* (New York: Fordham University Press, 2005) 5.

time.[17] And it does so through the efficacy of the sacramental relations. Following St. Augustine, a sacrament is an outward and visible sign of an inward and spiritual grace. It is a material means by which a spiritual reality is embodied and made present. Sacraments consist of words, such as blessings and benedictions; food, such as bread, wine, water, oil, and other material means, such as movements and gestures, by which the spiritual is mediated, embodied, given. This sacramental aspect of the liturgy is predicated upon the capacity of immanent matter to be a vehicle through which the transcendent spirit is embodied for our experience. And this experience is ultimately aesthetic. The aesthetic is the sacrament of the ethical. In fact, Pickstock argues that it is *only* in the liturgy that the aesthetic and ethical are held together.[18] For our recognition of this trace in the Other is indeed our "recognition," not through cognition, but through our senses, through sight, smell, touch. The author of the 34th Psalm says, "taste and see that the Lord is good." In the *Timaeus*, that most mystical of Plato's dialogues, which sets out to explore the origin of the cosmos, the Demiurge makes the cosmos as good and as beautiful as possible.[19] William Desmond observes, "The coming to form of the cosmos is an *aesthetic act* that affirms the *ontological good* of what comes to be. Not the horror of being, but the worthiness of being to be affirmed—this is what, one might almost say, is *sung*."[20] And it is singing, intonation, chant that marks the celebration of the liturgy. The sacrament works because it opens immanence

---

17. Pickstock argues that space and time are not merely opposed to one another, they are completely "dissolved," that is, "to be non-liturgical means to have got rid of the differentiations of time and space, and to live in a perpetual virtual space of identical repetition," 167. This is most definitely not what Kierkegaard meant by repetition.

18. Pickstock, "Liturgy, Art, and Politics," 163.

19. *Timaeus*, trans. B. Jowett, in *Plato: The Collected Dialogues*, Edith Hamilton and Huntington Cairns, eds. (Bollingen Foundation (Princeton: Princeton University Press, 1961) 29b, 1162.

20. William Desmond, *Art, Origins, Otherness: Between Philosophy and Art* (Albany: SUNY Press, 2003) 29.

to transcendence; it does not reject the latter for the former in a rationalist manner nor does it reject, in romantic fashion, the former for the latter. The sacramental nature of the liturgy speaks of the presence of the spiritual, of the transcendent right here, with us, through song. The heart and soul of the sacramental dimension of the liturgy is the icon. For Levinas, the icon is the trace of the Divine in the Other. Our obligation to the Other is due to the fact that the Other bears the trace of what is beyond being, call it the Good, the Divine, God. And as Plato observed in the *Timaeus*, "It is everyway necessary that the cosmos be an eikon of something."[21] And so it is to the icon, particularly as it is understood in the ancient practice of the Eastern Byzantine Christian tradition, that requires our attention.

III

In *Crossing the Visible* phenomenologist Jean-Luc Marion suggested, almost in passing, that the image-affirming doctrine of the Second Council of Nicaea concerns not only nor first of all a point in the history of ideas, nor even a decision of Christian dogma: it formulates above all and—perhaps the only—alternative to the contemporary disaster of the image. In the icon, the visible and the invisible embrace each other from a fire that no longer destroys but rather lights up the divine face for humanity.[22]

The icon is the visual, aesthetic manifestation of the porosity of being, of this "between" the material and spiritual, in which the material, the immanent, can indeed embody the spiritual, the transcendent. The icon, as argued by the Second Council of Nicaea in the eighth century, the seventh and last of the so-called Ecumenical Councils of the Church, is not merely an affirmation of art's ability to embody spiritual presence. It is the heart and soul of religion. All dogma, tradition, and practice are manifest in and through the veneration of the icon, which occurs in and

21. Ibid., 5.

22. Jean-Luc Marion, *Crossing the Visible*, trans. James K. A. Smith (Palo Alto, CA: Stanford University Press, 2002) 87.

through sound, smells, sacred space, gestures of bowing, touching, even kissing. The entire economy of the icon, including the philosophical thought that it generated by apologetics during the bitter iconoclastic controversies, critiques a dominant trend in Hellenistic philosophy that matter and spirit could never be mixed. The presence of the icon, its production and its reception—its use—testifies to the belief that the spiritual and material world can neither be opposed to nor cut off from each other. The religious worldview, as exemplified by the icon, marks the belief that salvation and redemption is never just "out there" but always "right here." (Religious fundamentalism, in whatever form, denies the liturgical essence of religion by sealing off the immanent from the transcendent in order to secure an utterly disembodied redemption in a world to come. It fears matter, immanence, believing that it *blocks* rather than opens to the spiritual and the transcendent.) Significantly, the Second Council of Nicaea rejected the notion that icons were merely of "educational" value, which was the preferred emphasis of the Latin Church (and which was further intensified by Luther). Rather, it asserted that the icon *projects* presence. It is a window through which the spiritual can be experienced in matter. It disciplines sight, as we look at the world through the eyes of faith, seeing the Other not as an instrument for our use but to whom something is owed, *who looks back at us.* An icon is a tool of "communication," an apparatus for "education" and "edification" in which a preformed thought, message, or meaning is wrapped in form and sent out to a viewer to be then unwrapped in order to "get" the message. It is not a visual illustration of a thought, message, or doctrine. It *is.* And it thus must be experienced, contemplated, participated with, even venerated. St. John of Damascus, one of the most important ninth-century defenders of icons, observes "Man is a microcosm; for he possesses a soul and a body, and is placed between spirit and matter; he is the place in which the visible and invisible creations, the tangible and intangible creations, are linked together."[23]

---

23. Quoted in John Meyendorff, *Christ in Eastern Christian Thought* (Crestwood, NY: St. Vladimir's Seminary Press, 1987) 161.

St. John's observation about humanity will be echoed time and again and not just by religious believers. Despite Nietzsche's hatred of a mushy, nineteenth-century Lutheran Christianity, Zarathustra's declarations that "Man is a rope stretched between the animal and the Overman—a rope over an abyss" and "man is a bridge not a goal—rejoicing over his noontides and evenings, as advances to new rosy dawns" seem frighteningly close to those of St. John of Damascus.[24] For both thinkers, humanity, by its very nature, always already traverses Lessing's "ugly broad ditch," a ditch that is the imaginative projection of Lessing's own lack of imagination. Pascal's rumination that "man is beyond man" and "humanity infinitely transcends humanity" echoes amongst both the saint of the Eastern Orthodox Church and the saint of postmodern nihilism.[25]

In a provocative speech, Fr. Pavel Florensky, Orthodox priest, scientist, art historian, theologian, and martyr, in his attempt to save the Russian Orthodox churches (and priests) from State destruction, describes in great detail the context within which the icon is intended to be experienced, which includes flickering candlelight illuminating the darkness of the sanctuary, the blue haze of incense, and the sounds of chanted prayer, an entire spatial apparatus that provides the framework for experiencing the icon in all its intended potential.[26] Reflection on the economy of the icon incorporates objects, processes, and environments into an expansive and comprehensive aesthetic framework that is the essence of the religious worldview, in which "belief" or "faith" is *practiced* through the sacrament and the liturgy; indeed, through the aesthetic. In the Eastern Orthodox Church, as it is for Judaism

24. Friedrich Nietzsche, *Thus Spoke Zarathustra: First Part*, in *The Portable Nietzsche*, Walter Kaufmann, ed. and trans. (New York: Penguin, 1982) first part, sec. 4, p. 126; 127.

25. Blaise Pascal, *Pensées*, Roger Ariew, ed. and trans. (Indianapolis: Hacket, 2005) 36.

26. Pavel Florensky, "The Church Ritual as Synthesis of the Arts" (1918), in *Beyond Vision: Essays on the Perception of Art*, Nicoletta Misler, ed. (London: Reaktion, 2002) 108.

and Islam, even the Holy Scriptures and the Creed are *sung*. As poet Joseph Brodsky observed, "Song is, after all, restructured Time, toward which mute Space is inherently hostile."[27] And "mute Space," devoid of the sacred offered by the liturgy, is the distinctive achievement of the Enlightenment, which Pickstock calls "spatialization," a dissolving of time and space into a nondescript "fixed and perpetual place."[28]

IV

Much contemporary artistic practice, however, not only senses the presence of the religious, but it is also sensitive to the liturgical and sacramental dimension of human life and work.[29] While Pickstock argues for the necessity of "a liturgical understanding of art," she decries avant-garde art as a "sham mode of liturgy."[30] Contra Pickstock, I would like to suggest that the problem lies less with artistic practice than with critical practice, it is precisely the lack of sensitivity to the liturgical and sacramental that is symptomatic of an anti-religious projection on the part of too many modern art critics. It is not artistic practice that is a "sham," it is its "understanding," it is its criticism.[31] Critical practice either actively denies the presence of the religious in modern and contemporary art or embraces the most tepid and over romanticized notions of "spirituality" to give contemporary art a "higher" purpose.

Art criticism must move beyond the modernist reductions that deny the relationship between artistic and religious practice,

27. Joseph Brodsky, "Introduction," *Osip Mandelstam: 50 Poems* (New York: Persea, 1977) 16.

28. Pickstock, "Liturgy, Art, and Politics," 178.

29. For a more detailed analysis of contemporary artistic practice from a liturgical and sacramental worldview, see my *God in the Gallery: A Christian Embrace of Modern Art* (Grand Rapids: Baker Academic, 2008).

30. Pickstock, "Liturgy, Art, and Politics," 165; 164.

31. For an in depth discussion of art criticism in this context, see my *God in the Gallery*, 109–31.

between the aesthetic and the ethical, between the beautiful and the good. It must do so by embracing the liturgical nature of both art and religion and acknowledging the necessity of belief for both practices to work. A critical perspective that is nourished by the aesthetic dimensions and philosophical implications of the liturgical, sacramental, and iconic can accommodate the implicit, intuitive, and even unconscious religious practices of much contemporary art, picking up on its echoes and reverberations. In many ways, like philosophy, art is religion pursued by other means. And I suggest that there is a deep relationship between aesthetic and ascetic practice, between the disciplines of artistic and religious practice, which the language of art criticism is incapable of perceiving. Art criticism must, in some way, be true to the richness of experience, which includes religious experience, which is mediated in and through the liturgy. It testifies aesthetically to the porosity of being, to its excesses and "too muchness," that constitutes the "between" of self and Other. Artistic practice is an aesthetic intuition of the religious, an intuition that often transcends the artist's own self-understanding of their work. Theological and philosophical reflection on religious practice, from liturgy and sacrament to the economy of the icon, offers vast resources for an expansive art criticism that can most creatively accommodate contemporary artistic practice. Perhaps one of the most poignant examples of liturgical expression in contemporary literature comes from Cormac McCarthy's *The Road.*

> The boy sat tottering. The man watched him that he not topple into the flames. He kicked holes in the sand for the boy's hips and shoulders where he would sleep and he sat holding him while he tousled his hair before the fire to dry it. All of this like some ancient anointing. So be it. Evoke the forms. Where you've nothing else construct ceremonies out of the air and breathe upon them.[32]

We are liturgical creatures. Contemporary artistic practice recognizes this. It is time that critical practice do the same.

32. Cormac McCarthy, *The Road* (New York: Knopf, 2006) 63. I owe this reference and its liturgical nature to James K. A. Smith.

2

Linda Montano and the Tensions of Monasticism

Karen Gonzalez Rice

In an early action, *Happiness Piece* (1973), performance artist Linda Montano photographed herself smiling every-day: "I wanted the habit of happiness to be available to me so I disciplined myself to smile everyday."[1] This simple piece calls attention to Montano's lifelong performance commitments: the discipline of a daily vow; the cultivation of an outward appearance that, in turn, fosters inner conditions; and her concern with unhappiness, particularly suffering.

In this essay, I theorize Montano's performance art in terms of her experience as a novice in the Maryknoll Catholic convent between 1960 and 1962. In order to explore the ways in which conceptual and bodily practices of monasticism are manifested in her performance actions, I address Montano's collaborative performance with artist Tehching Hsieh, *Art / Life: One Year Performance*, in which she and Hsieh remained tied together by an eight-foot rope for one year (1983 to 1984), and *7 Years of Living Art* (1984–1991), a performance that highlighted the activities of daily life as art. Ultimately, I will suggest that Montano's performance actions enact the commitments of and certain tensions within monasticism.[2]

---

1. Linda Montano, *Art in Everyday Life* (Los Angeles: Astro Artz, 1981) 25.

2. Montano herself prefers the term "convent life" to monasticism.

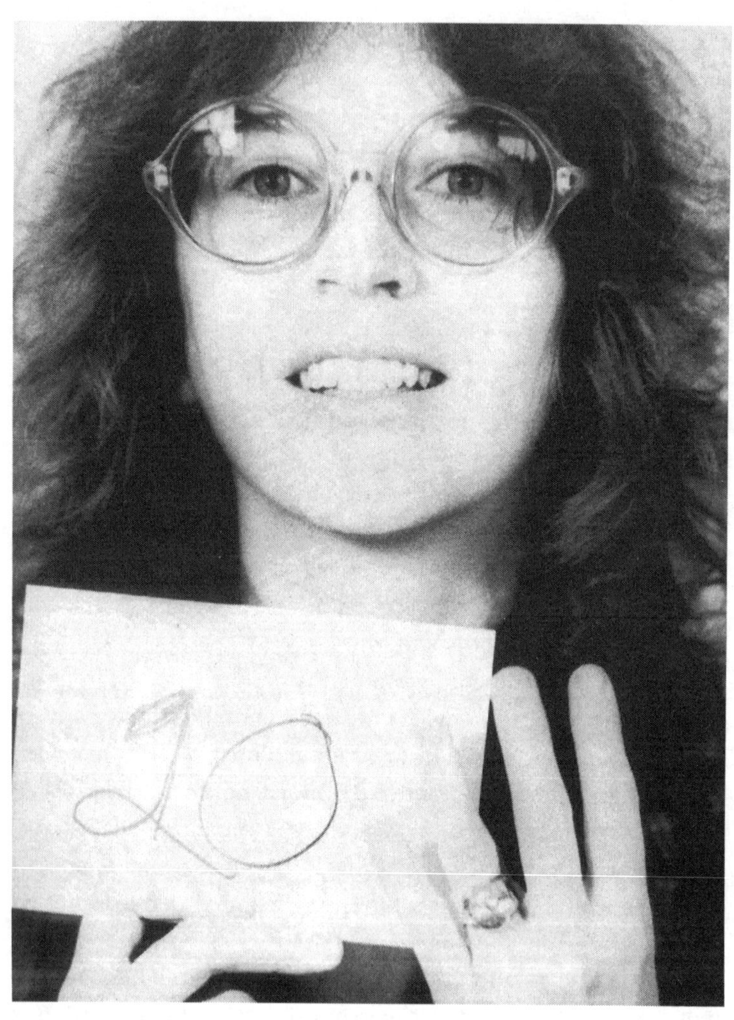

FIGURE 1: Linda Montano, *Happiness Piece*, 1973.

Montano consistently frames her art in terms of religion: "I literally took the smells of church, the sights of church, the sounds of church, and almost, as if speaking another language, translated those into my work."[3] In many performances she explicitly mentions Catholicism, enacts Catholic rituals, or takes on her Maryknoll name, Sister Rose Augustine.[4] Other art actions draw directly on her varied experiences, between 1970 and 1998, as student and practitioner of Eastern religious traditions, including Zen Buddhism and Hinduism.[5] Despite this spiritual complexity, she consistently has verbalized her religious commitments in Catholic language, actions, and metaphors, and I focus here on the specifically Catholic resonances of her performance works. While descriptions of Montano's work mention her interest in and connection with religion, this issue has not been adequately explored by art historians. Even Eleanor Heartney, who directly addresses the issue of Catholicism in contemporary art, provides only a cursory interpretation of the Catholic nature of Montano's work.[6]

With her deliberate experiments at the borders between art and life, Montano insists on autobiography as a critical element of her art; thus, my exploration of her work begins with a study of

3. Linda M. Montano, *Letters from Linda M. Montano*, ed. Jennie Klein (New York: Routledge, 2005) 60.

4. These include *Learning to Talk* (1977); year six (1989–1990) of *7 Years of Living Art* (1984–1991); and the workshop collaboration *Saint Summer Camp 1987* (1987).

5. Montano's enduring interest in Eastern religious traditions began with her study of yoga in 1970. In addition, she lived in a Buddhist monastery for many years, studied Hindi traditions to become a *sanyasi*, and traveled to India in 1997. I further explore the relationship between Montano's Catholic, Buddhist, and Hindi experiences of monasticism and the impact of these monastic traditions on her art in my dissertation, "Self-Sacrifice, Traumatic Experience, and Religion in the Performance Art of Linda Montano, John Duncan, and Ron Athey (forthcoming, Duke University). See also *The Third Mind: American Artists Contemplate Asia, 1860 to 1989* (New York: Guggenheim, 2009).

6. Eleanor Heartney, *Postmodern Heretics: The Catholic Imagination in Contemporary Art* (New York: Midmarch Arts Press, 2004) 54–57.

her biography.[7] Born in 1942 in Saugerties, New York, Montano was educated in Catholic schools in her childhood, attended church with her family, and "wanted to be a saint."[8] She entered the Maryknoll convent as a novice in 1960. She describes this experience lovingly, as an "incredibly rich time," but she became anorexic and left the order in 1962.[9] After her recovery, she attended the College of New Rochelle in New York, where a nun encouraged her work in art, and she began to create life-size sculptures of the Crucifixion. She studied sculpture in Italy in 1965 and earned her MFA in sculpture from the University of Wisconsin-Madison in 1969.

Montano began creating art actions during her time in graduate school. Intimidated by her male colleagues, who were working on large-scale Minimalist sculpture, and embarrassed by her religiously-focused work, she began to exhibit and perform with chickens. For Montano, the nervous, erratic behaviors of chickens manifested her own anxieties and restlessness: "I was combining the image of a live chicken, and being a chicken, being a person, being a nun . . ."[10] Ultimately, she worked with this chicken theme for over a decade in works such as *Lying: Dead Chicken-Live Angel* (1971). Of these early performances Montano has written, "I was getting the kind of attention that I used to give to nuns, priests, saints, statues, crucifixes, etc. I had reversed religion for myself."[11]

It is important to note that in the 1970s art scene, the medium of performance art was—as it remains today—a mar-

---

7. This brief biographical sketch is drawn from the following sources in which Montano discusses her past: Montano, *Letters from Linda M. Montano.*; Linda Montano, "Spirituality and Art," *Women Artists' News* 10/3 (1985); and her resume at http://www.bobsart.org/montano/more/vita.html.

8. Montano, *Letters from Linda M. Montano*, 18, 123.

9. Ibid., 18. For a thorough consideration of Montano's art in terms of the affect of trauma, and particularly her art's visual relationship to religion, representation, and traumatic experiences in her life, see my dissertation.

10. Montano, *Art in Everyday Life*, 86.

11. Ibid., 7.

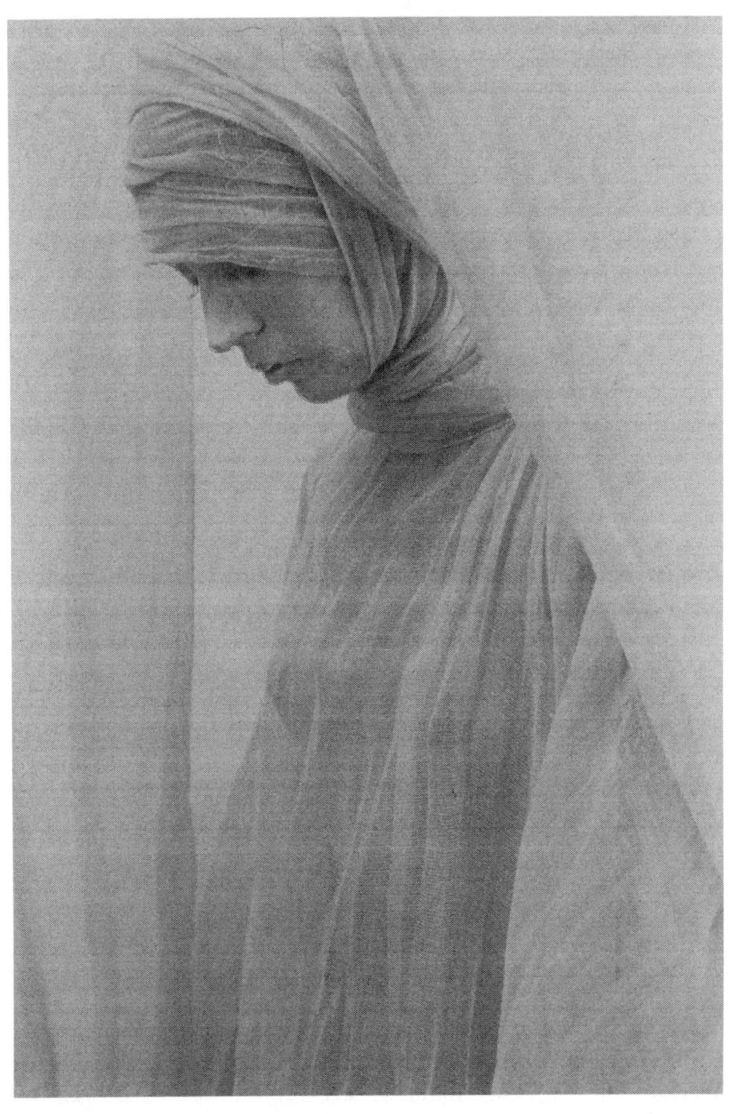

FIGURE 2: Linda Montano, *Lying: Dead Chicken, Live Angel*, 1971.

ginalized art activity. As an art practice, performance art (also called body art) developed in the aftermath of World War II. In response to the Holocaust, the atomic bomb, and other unspeakable experiences, artists—trained as painters and sculptors—felt that painting and sculpture were inadequate to express their experiences and instead began to create art actions. As a medium that privileges action-oriented, non-object art, performance art operates outside of the market and outside of traditional spaces of art. In addition, performance art posits an ambiguous distinction between performer and performance and between art and life—as Montano makes clear in her work.

In the early 1970s, Montano met and married Mitchell Payne, a photographer and former Presbyterian seminarian. In 1972, the couple moved to San Francisco, where Montano performed extensively. Over the next few years, she became a key figure in the California performance art scene, collaborating with Tom Marioni and performing at the Woman's Building in Los Angeles. Montano separated from Payne in 1975 and moved to San Diego to be with her new partner, composer Pauline Oliveros. In 1977, Payne died in an accidental shooting; Montano's grief is documented in *Mitchell's Death* (1979). Shortly after this traumatic event, in 1981, Montano and Pauline moved to the Zen Mountain Monastery in Mt. Tremper, New York—near her hometown of Saugerties.[12] She lived in this monastery for two years, leaving only after she saw the work of Tehching Hsieh and decided to collaborate with him in *Art / Life: One Year Performance* (1983–1984). This piece brought her to prominence in the New York art scene, and she began teaching performance art while simultaneously performing *7 Years of Living Art* (1984–1991), followed by *Another 7 Years of Living Art* (1991–1998). After short engagements at Ohio State University, UCLA, the Chicago Institute of Art, and others, she accepted a long-term teaching position at the University of Texas at Austin. In 1998, following a

12. Montano regularly returned to the Zen Mountain Monastery to live part-time or full time between 1984 and 1991.

painful struggle over tenure, Montano returned to her home in upstate New York to care for her ailing father. She transformed this task into an ongoing piece entitled *Dad Art* (1998–2004): "I have switched from being tied for a year with a rope . . . to being tied to the position of being Dad's advocate and caregiver."[13] At the same time, she returned to Catholicism: "I practice Roman Catholicism now because I feel I'm imprinted . . . But now I have enough skill to divide, to take out of the meal the things I can't eat and still be true to those incredible sacramental mysteries."[14] Her most recent works explicitly engage with Catholic themes and content, including pilgrimages to Catholic holy sites in Europe, the United States, and Latin America (2006); prayer pieces such as *A Silent Three-Hour Prayer Retreat Inside St. Patrick's Cathedral* (2007), and reenactments of the lives of saints and famous women religious, as in *Teresa of Avila* (2007).

I suggest that Montano's extensive engagement with Catholicism in her work pivots on her experience as a novice in the Maryknoll convent. She is reticent about her time there but emphasizes it as joyous, despite and perhaps including its traumatic elements: "At twenty I entered a convent, 'enduring' two years as a Catholic nun, living in silence those two years except for one hour a day when we all talked together in recreation. I loved the community and dedication to a higher good and absolutely pure goal, but I left anorexic, having lost nearly 50 pounds in six months, high as a kite on endorphins."[15]

Montano's experience traces broader trends relating to Catholic women religious at mid-century. She entered the Maryknoll convent in 1960, at a time when the population of women religious approached its height in the United States. This popula-

---

13. Montano, *Letters from Linda M. Montano*, 199.

14. Hilary Robinson, "God! I Love Time: An Interview with Linda Montano," *n.paradoxa* 5 (2000) 70.

15. Montano, *Letters from Linda M. Montano*, 123. There is a discrepancy of dates here: if Montano entered the convent in 1960, she would have been eighteen, not twenty.

tion reached its peak in 1965; between 1950 and 1966, the number of women religious increased by twenty-five percent, 147,000 to 181,421.[16] At the same time that these orders were successfully recruiting women, convents were experiencing increased rates of defection. In 1950, 381 novices did not take their final vows; in 1965, 1,562 of these women left their orders.[17]

Montano's experience of the Maryknoll convent took place before the Second Ecumenical Council of the Vatican (Vatican II), which in the early 1960s instituted revolutionary changes in Catholic practice concerning lay participation, the use of the vernacular rather than Latin in conducting Mass, and other significant issues. Vatican II profoundly impacted the lives of women religious in terms of participation, democracy, and laity interactions. However, long before the 1960s, traditions, rules, and attitudes that had been operating in Catholic convents for centuries were already in the process of changing. Vatican II addressed and codified the Church's response to issues that had been contested for decades.[18] The activities of the Maryknoll Sisters in particular participated in inciting this shift. Founded in 1911 by Mary Josephine Rogers (Mother Mary Joseph), the order was devoted to missionary work. Montano entered the convent in 1960 expecting to "go to Africa and cure leprosy, or to China and do something similarly dramatic."[19] In addition to this missionary focus, the Maryknoll order established a cloister in 1932 to support sisters interested in pursuing contemplative lives.[20] For Mother Mary Joseph, isolation and encounter were

16. Helen Rose Fuchs Ebaugh, *Women in the Vanishing Cloister: Organizational Decline in Catholic Religious Orders in the United States* (New Brunswick, NJ: Rutgers University Press, 1993) 1.

17. Ibid., 50. Like other organizations in the United States, the American Catholic church grew dramatically in 1950s and early 1960s, only to decline sharply in late the 1960s and 1970s.

18. Lora Ann Quinonez and Mary Daniel Turner, *The Transformation of American Catholic Sisters* (Philadelphia: Temple University Press, 1992) 3-4.

19. Montano, "Spirituality and Art," 8.

20. Barbara Hendricks, "The Legacy of Mary Josephine Rogers," *International Bulletin of Missionary Research* 21 (1997) 7.

complementary activities within the order: "a missioner must be a contemplative in action."[21] She described Maryknoll nuns' responsibilities as follows: "Sisters shall be encouraged to undertake direct catechetical and evangelical work and for that purpose will expect to go from station to station for visitations comparable to those of the priests."[22]

This concept of missionary action, known as the direct apostolate, represented a significant shift from conventional practice. Maryknoll sisters in China were the first nuns to receive permission to evangelize rather than simply to provide social services to indigenous peoples. With these new priorities, restrictions on nuns were relaxed: the sisters wore modified habits to ride bicycles, and rather than returning to the cloister each evening, they could live with families in remote villages.[23] This flexible, highly successful approach drew large numbers of postulants. By 1960, the Maryknoll order was sending more missionary sisters overseas than any other Catholic organization. According to the Catholic Mission Association, they supported 555 separate institutes in countries across Asia, Latin America, and Africa, while the organization with the next-most missionary sisters supported only 168 institutes.[24]

21. Ibid., 6.

22. Ibid.

23. Angelyn Dries, "American Catholic "Woman's Work for Woman" in the Twentieth Century," in *Gospel Bearers, Gender Barriers: Missionary Women in the Twentieth Century*, ed. Dana L. Robert (Maryknoll: Orbis, 2002) 140. Maryknoll nuns' participation in the direct apostolate occurred due to the urging of Bishop Francis Ford in China's Kaying province. The nuns adopted common practices of lay evangelization in China at the time (Dries, "American Catholic 'Woman's Work for Woman' in the Twentieth Century," 139.)

24. Dries, "American Catholic 'Woman's Work for Woman' in the Twentieth Century," 130. Due to their flexible, embedded, intersubjective missionary practices already in place, the Maryknoll order was less troubled than other orders by Vatican II. Many present-day Maryknoll sisters embrace social and political activism; for example, they are highly involved in Latin American civil society and social movements. See Bernice Kita, "Maryknoll Sisters in Latin America 1943–1993," *Missiology* 26/4 (1998).

Montano was profoundly influenced by the activities and structures of daily life in the Maryknoll convent. Pre-Vatican II Catholic convent communities, including Maryknoll, were distinguished from lay or secular communities by three key features: discipline, collaboration (as a commitment to living in community), and the integration of life and prayer.[25] In particular, female monasticism was characterized by an almost complete lack of privacy. While outsiders generally perceive monasticism as an experience of isolation and seclusion, these women lived in constant community. Communal living in dormitories, uniform dress—for novices, a modified form of the habit—and a routinized daily schedule separated novices from their communities of origin in order to constantly reinforce a sense of religious identity and belonging to the convent community.[26] Obedience to superiors was crucial—insisted upon even in nuns' vows—and supported by the supernatural origin of their authority. All aspects of life were open to the approval or disapproval of the convent leadership. For example, nuns and novices were allowed to leave the physical space of the convent only with permission, and then only in the company of another nun.[27] In this way, a scaffolding of social support organized interactions with the outside world, representing and asserting the convent community's beliefs and practices against any outside pressures. Thus the communities created within convents were socially as well as architecturally cloistered.

In this experience of living in community, discipline emerges as a central tension. In the form of the vow, discipline presents itself as a question of will: one must constantly choose to fulfill it. The novice must cultivate this discipline through an extreme willingness to collaborate—to stretch her self-perception by

25. Some features of this distinction between religious and lay communities are suggested by Ebaugh, *Women in the Vanishing Cloister: Organizational Decline in Catholic Religious Orders in the United States*, 89.

26. Ibid., 90.

27. Ibid., 24.

identifying wholly with the community. Discipline thus becomes intimately linked to collaboration. At the same time, collaboration clashes with the notion of a contemplative life. It is important to note that a life of meditation and prayer isolates members of the convent community from the outside world, but not from each other. In particular, missionary work, as an alternative collaborative project, challenges this insider dynamic by calling for sustained, active engagement with outsider-others. Devotion to missionary work and to the contemplative life require different, but equally extreme, forms of collaboration. Coming out of her convent experience, Montano internalized these two forms of collaboration to the extent that: "in order to stay alive and out of the mental hospital and give myself the energy I needed to live, I had to do public actions because there was no sense of me outside of the other. There was no sense of me outside my action done. I was meaningless unless I was the other."[28] I suggest that Montano's performance actions reflect and enact the tensions within her own experience of monasticism with the Maryknoll sisters. By calling attention to the tensions of monasticism, I do not necessarily refer to contradictions, the juxtaposition of opposites, or unrecognized or sublimated conflict. Instead, I draw on the definition of tension as an "act of stretching" and as "balancing forces causing extension."[29] Monastic life—the creation of an intentional community—explicitly addresses issues involved in living in community as a means to spiritual growth or extension. Thus my use of "tension" in the monastic context suggests a non-evaluative attention to the productive negotiations of living in community. These may be more or less contradictory, more or less conflictual, more or less resolvable, and more or less healthy, but they always involve commitment, extension, and expansion of the self and the community.

28. Robinson, "God! I Love Time: An Interview with Linda Montano," 64.

29. Kristine Stiles, "Performance," in *Critical Terms for Art History*, ed. Robert Nelson and Richard Shiff (Chicago: University of Chicago Press, 2003).

In the remainder of this essay, I argue that Linda Montano's work enacts the tensions within monasticism, the stretching and extension of the self that occurs through a commitment to collaboration and living in community. In particular, I address two key performances— Montano's collaborative performance with Tehching Hsieh, *Art / Life: One Year Performance* (1983–1984) and *7 Years of Living Art* (1984–1991) to explore the ways in which her performance art calls attention to and attempts to come to terms with fundamental elements of monastic life: the vow and its visual marker, the habit; collaboration; and, finally, suffering.

Art / Life: One Year Performance took place in Manhattan between 1983 and 1984.[30] Montano was attracted by the "rigor" of Hsieh's endurance-based artistic practices, and in order to work with him, she left the Zen monastery where she had lived for two years:[31] "I was living in a Zen Center in upstate New York and during a trip to the city I saw one of Tehching's posters and literally heard a voice in my head that said, 'Do a one-year piece with him.'"[32] In another account of her decision to collaborate with Hsieh, Montano makes the vocational aspect of her decision explicit: "Although I would have preferred to have stayed in the monastery, I knew that my calling was to be a fringe, outsider artist."[33]

As a collaboration between two artists, *Art / Life: One Year Performance* drew on themes from both Hsieh's and Montano's

30. This image, photographed on October 18, 1983, can also be found in Tehching Heieh and Adrian Heathfield, *Out of Now: The Lifeworks of Tehching Hsieh* (Cambridge, MA: MIT Press, 2009) 249.

31. Alex Grey and Allyson Grey, "Linda Montano and Tehching Hsieh's One Year Performance: Alex and Allyson Grey Ask Question about the Year of the Rope," *High Performance* 7 n. 3 (1984) 25.

32. Ibid.

33. Robinson, "God! I Love Time: An Interview with Linda Montano," 67. I use the term "vocation" in the Weberian sense of *Beruf*, which indicates an occupational calling dictated by God (Max Weber, *The Protestant Ethic and the "Spirit" of Capitalism and Other Writings* (New York: Penguin, 2002 [1905], 109.)

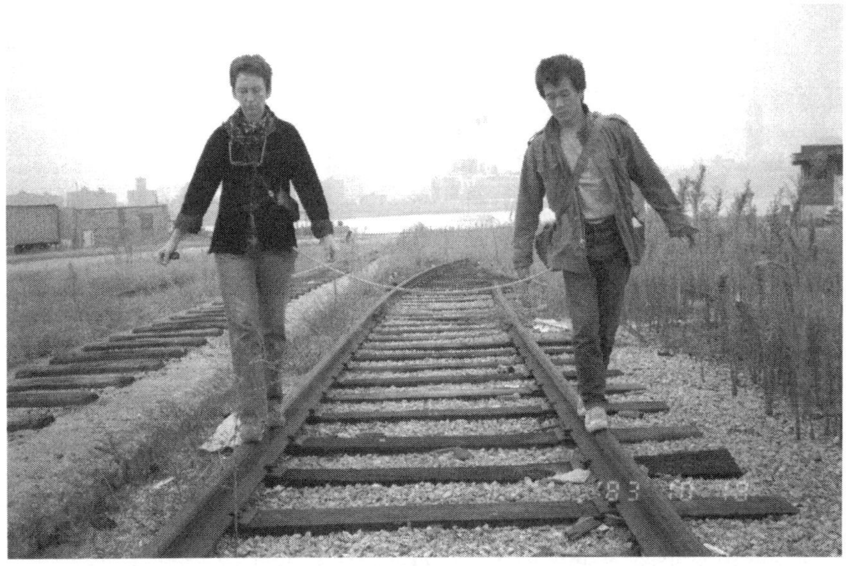

FIGURE 3: Tehching Hsieh, Linda Montano, *Art/Life One Year Performance 1983–1984.*

past work. The title of the piece illustrates the influence of each artist's investments. "One Year Performance" repeats the title that Hsieh used for all of his performance pieces between 1978 and 1986. These endurance works included living in a cage for one year, punching a time card every hour for one year, and living outdoors for one year.[34] The phrase "Art / Life" directly references Montano's small business / long-running performance piece, *Art-Life Counseling* (begun in 1980) as well as previous collaborative pieces in which she attempted to blur the boundary between art and life. These include *Handcuff* (1973), a three-day collaboration with Tom Marioni in which the artists remained handcuffed to one another for three days, and several works performed with Pauline Oliveros in 1975, such as *Living with Pauline Oliveros in the Desert for Ten Days* and *Living Art*. In these pieces, Oliveros

34. Tehching Hsieh, *Tehching Hsieh: One Year Performance Art Documents 1978–1999* (2000).

37

and Montano designated that "everything we did would be considered art."[35]

Art / Life: One Year Performance established a set of promises or assertions which bound Montano and Hsieh. In the form of a signed contract, this vow stipulated that the artists would remain tied together with an eight foot rope for one year, without touching. When inside, Hsieh and Montano would be in the same room. In effect, this vow created a monastic community of two. In literally tying the two artists together, the eight-foot rope connecting Hsieh and Montano functioned as the vow itself; but it also visually marked the vow. In this sense, the rope became both vow and habit.[36] It enacted the convent practice of leaving the cloister with at least one other nun: the artists and everyone who came into contact with them were constantly confronted with the physicality of the vow.[37] In an interview conducted during this piece, Montano described the discipline of the vow as a kind of separation of the will from the mind and the body: "once you give the mind a command, then you watch the body carry out the process."[38] This observational attitude was echoed in the extensive documentation of the piece. The artists photographed their daily activities and recorded all conversations. Any deviation from the rules (accidental touching, for example) was rigorously documented in photographs and narratives.[39]

35. Montano, *Art in Everyday Life*, 54.

36. Hsieh and Montano shaved their heads on the first day of the piece and did not cut their hair throughout the year, echoing Buddhist and some Christian monastic practices.

37. The use of the rope as abstracted habit in *Art / Life: One Year Performance* recalls Montano's practice of wearing a nun's habit in her earliest performance piece, *Lying: Dead Chicken, Live Angel* (1971) and repeated throughout her early career in works such as *Sitting: Dead Chicken, Live Angel* (1971), *The Screaming Nun* (1975), *Learning to Talk* (1977) and *Listening to the 80s: Inside/Outside* (1980) as well as in the recent video work *Teresa of Avila* (2007).

38. Grey and Grey, "Linda Montano and Tehching Hsieh's One Year Performance: Alex and Allyson Grey Ask Question about the Year of the Rope," 27.

39. Montano came to believe that this extensive documentation ultimately failed to adequately capture the piece: "It seems that the primary document

Art / Life: One Year Performance required an extreme degree of intimacy and trust. As in the convent (or in a cage), the two were absolutely restricted from privacy. Each action, comment, and gesture could be observed by the other. In addition, any decision required extensive discussion. Each day, Montano and Hsieh spent approximately five hours at desks, back to back. They used this time to make decisions about their daily activities: "We think about what we want to do and then we talk until we come to a consensus. So it takes many hours of sitting before we can do one thing."[40] In the duration of the piece, Montano became interested in documenting the inevitable conflicts that took place between them.[41] She felt that this tension was an integral aspect of the piece, a working-out of the problems of living in community. Hsieh, on the other hand, considered the piece a formal exercise and was extremely resistant to personal, social, or political interpretations. Over time, the artists began to vent their anger over their differences of theoretical point of view as well as daily trivialities. Conflicts arose over what and where to eat, how and when to contact friends and art critics, and how to manage the demands of their jobs (Hsieh was doing carpentry work and Montano was teaching). Eventually, "yanking [became] a chief mode of expressing anger."[42]

This violence speaks to the difficulty of the vow and the difficulty of the commitment to living in community. Montano framed the experience in terms of cultivating humility through the painful and problematic discipline of collaboration: "By staying tied to Tehching Hsieh in his *Art/Life: One Year Performance,*

---

is the change inside the performer and the audience. The results are felt and cannot always be photographed or expressed" (ibid., 29.).

40. Ibid., 26.

41. Many of the conflicts arose in relation to differing gender expectations. In particular, Hsieh, a carpenter, refused to allow Montano to help him with his carpentry jobs, which angered her (Jill Johnston, "Hardship Art," *Art in America* 72 n. 8 [1984] 179).

42. Ibid.

I died a little every day, learning humility and collaboration."[43] Montano's emphasis on the death of the self in this quote calls attention to the role of suffering and self-inflicted hardship in the piece. Critics and art historians have argued that this work did not approximate the kind of physical danger that Chris Burden or Vito Acconci set up in their endurance work. However, this view does not account for the psychological (and occasional physical) risk that accompanied this project. As Hsieh said, "We become each other's cage."[44] Completing the piece without the loss of the psychic self became Montano's priority. Conflict management thus equaled survival: "For survival we have to work things out."[45] Yet the performance of vulnerability and suffering also relates to the mitigation of long-term fears and anxieties. For Montano, discipline through collaboration serves as a kind of preparation for future hardship: "I do hard work in case life gets hard. Then I will be ready."[46]

Self-denial continues to characterize the subsequent works of both Montano and Hsieh, even to the present. In 2000, Hsieh completed a thirteen-year project entitled *Earth*, in which he made art but did not show it publicly or communicate about it at all. Most recently, Montano vowed to renounce writing, an activity that she loves, for seven years beginning in 2004.[47]

While tied to Hsieh, Montano conceived a plan for her next performance, *7 Years of Living Art* (1984–1991). In this long-

43. Montano, *Letters from Linda M. Montano*, 245. Despite their equal conception of and participation in the work, Montano in recent years usually has referred to the piece as Hsieh's (for example, in Montano, *Letters from Linda M. Montano*, 58, 66, 164.).

44. Grey and Grey, "Linda Montano and Tehching Hsieh's One Year Performance: Alex and Allyson Grey Ask Question about the Year of the Rope," 25.

45. Ibid., 27.

46. Robinson, "God! I Love Time: An Interview with Linda Montano," 67.

47. The idea that one's gifts or talents may be dangerously self-glorifying can be found in other individuals within monastic communities, such as the monk / writer Thomas Merton, who had to be convinced by his order to continue writing.

term piece, Montano continued her experiments in combining art and life activities. She established a set of prescriptions which structured her life on an annual, monthly, and daily basis: each year of the piece corresponded to one of the seven Hindi chakras and was associated with one color and one of seven personas. Montano drew on personas that she originally had created in an early video work, *Learning to Talk* (1977)—including the character of a nun with her Maryknoll name, Sister Rose Augustine.[48] In *7 Years of Living Art*, Montano explicitly engaged with Hindi symbolism; but she also referenced Catholic metaphors of the seven sacraments, the seven sorrows, and others. The structure of the piece itself echoed monastic organization: Montano designated three sets of commitments, inner, outer, and others. Daily vows or "inner" commitments included wearing only clothing of the year's color, spending at least three hours in a room of that color, listening to one tone for seven hours each day, and speaking in an accent associated with the persona of the year.[49] Here, as in *Art / Life: One Year Performance*, Montano created a visual marker of the vow that also functioned as a habit in terms of the practice of assuming clothing and accents. As part of the "outer" commitments of this piece, Montano held monthly one-on-one Art-Life counseling sessions at the New Museum. In addition, each year she hosted one or more artist collaborators ("others") in her home for sixteen days.[50] Thus, the piece incorporated

48. Montano, *Letters from Linda M. Montano*, xii. This multiplication and fragmentation of the self is one of the many marks of trauma in Montano's work, which I explore further in my dissertation.

49. Robinson, "God! I Love Time: An Interview with Linda Montano," 68. Montano's work consistently calls attention to clothing, fashion, and modeling. The acts of changing clothes, wearing all of her clothes, or being photographed in different outfits figures prominently in pieces such as *Husband-Wife Fashion Show* (1974), *Learning to Talk* (1977), and *7 Years of Living Art* (1984–1991). These works recall Bas Jan Ader's *All My Clothes* (1970) and Charles Ray's *All My Clothes* (1973).

50. For several years, these collaborators were Annie Sprinkle and Veronica Vera. See, for example, Linda Montano, Annie Sprinkle, and Veronica Vera, "Summer Saint Camp 1987: With Annie Sprinkle and Veronica Vera," *The Drama Review: TDR* 33 (1989).

seclusion—in the cloister of the one-color room and the daily "inner" disciplines—and its "outer" and "other" complement, missionary work. In particular, Montano's uniquely Maryknoll approach to collaboration in the confessional space of the New Museum consultations and her in-home workshops echoes the direct apostolate, the missionary practice of directly engaging with individuals around spiritual issues.[51]

I believe that Montano's attitude toward suffering changed during *7 Years of Living Art*. While still essentially concerned with self-denial, it seems that in the performance of this piece, Montano learned some flexibility within the vow: "[I was] so S&M-ish, so disciplined, so difficult on myself that after the third year . . . all the disciplines fell away and it became a fashion statement." She no longer assumed accents in speaking, but she did continue to wear single-colored clothing, enact some interior practices, and conduct her New Museum work and collaborative workshops.[52] At the same time, this piece clarifies Montano's investment in purity. In her early work, created just after leaving the convent in the midst of her struggle with anorexia, Montano explicitly connected the medium of performance to purity: "I didn't want to make more things . . . the invisible, sculpting the invisible, seemed less polluting and more *arte povera*."[53] As *7 Years of Living Art* progressed, Montano decided that "my priority now is to be at-

51. During *7 Years of Living Art*, these physical, behavioral activities constituted Montano's "inner" work. However, in her continuation of the piece, *Another 7 Years of Living Art* (1991–1998), Montano redefined these rules: clothing colors and listening to a single sound became "outer" rather than "inner" commitments, and she defined her inner work as increasing her attention to spiritual matters. This echoes the shift from postulate to novice, or from novice to nun, when habits of speech, dress, and schedule are maintained but de-emphasized in favor of more abstract forms of spiritual commitment.

52. This attention to the long-term sustainability of her performance vows was fine-tuned in *Another 7 Years of Living Art*: Montano allowed herself to fulfill her "other" commitment—annual visits to the United Nations Chagall Chapel in New York—by "sit[ting there] physically or astrally" (Montano, *Letters from Linda M. Montano*, 166).

53. Robinson, "God! I Love Time: An Interview with Linda Montano," 67.

tentive, natural and pure enough in heart to walk in the snow and enjoy it."[54] Montano's phrasing echoes the Sermon on the Mount: "Blessed are the pure in heart, for they shall see God."[55]

Of her early work Montano has written, "My primary concern in most events was to become a presence (Catholic saint) via self imposed disciplines."[56] Throughout her work, Montano consistently explores the tensions and "self imposed disciplines" inherent in monastic life. Through her commitment to the vow and to the discipline of collaboration, Montano makes visible the constant negotiations of living in community and the painful process of the expansion of the self.

54. Montano, "Spirituality and Art," 8.

55. Matthew, *Beatitudes*. Montano's search for purity through endurance and self-deprivation resonates with Buddhist ascetic traditions as well as her traumatic subjectivity. These subjects, elaborated in my dissertation, are crucial aspects of Montano's work, which complement and complicate the relationship of her art to Catholicism.

56. Montano, *Art in Everyday Life*, 87 (artist's parenthesis).

3

Theology and Art in the Postmodern Desert

Jason A. Danner

A THEOLOGICAL DEMUR

ARTISTS AND THEOLOGIANS ALIKE would have occasion to cheer the reemergence of a theological dimension in contemporary art. By overcoming their estrangement, art and theology could reenter a partnership that had been a great and singular boon.[1] But for certain theologians such a rapprochement must happen on theology's terms and not on art's. They contend that for art to express the revelation of transcendence as theology does it will have to go beyond the Kantian aesthetics of the sublime and allow for a manifestation of God who is radically and irreducibly transcendent to the human subject. Thus, art must do more than acknowledge the theological dimension in *it*: it will have to understand itself as situated *within* theology.

Such is the position John Milbank, Graham Ward and Catherine Pickstock take in their introduction to 1999's *Radical Orthodoxy*, the first publication by the influential Cambridge movement of the same name. For them, rethinking the relationship between art and theology is part of a broader critique of

---

1. Iris Murdoch remarked, "Christian art had the last theological word." Noted in Richard Viladesau, *Theological Aesthetics: God in Imagination, Beauty and Art* (Oxford: Oxford University Press, 1999) 186.

44

secular postmodern thought. As they see it, our postmodern situation is a desert of soulless nihilism left in the wake of the collapse of secular thought,[2] and as such presents an opportunity to "reclaim the world by situating its concerns and activities within a theological framework." Among these concerns: politics, sex, the body, personhood, visibility, space, and aesthetics. All of these are to be rescued from the autonomy granted them by secular thought by re-placement within a theological framework because, aver Milbank et al., *only* a theological framework can secure their coherence and resist "nihilistic drift" by restoring a sense of the world's participation in a sacred reality:

> The central theological framework of radical orthodoxy is "participation" as developed by Plato and reworked by Christianity, because any alternative configuration perforce reserves a territory independent of God. The latter can lead only to nihilism. Participation, however, refuses any reserve of created territory, while allowing finite things their own integrity . . . every discipline must be framed by a theological perspective; otherwise these disciplines will define a zone apart from God, grounded literally in nothing. Although it might seem that to treat of diverse worldly phenomena such as language, the body, aesthetic experience, political community, friendship, etc. apart from God is to safeguard their worldliness, in fact, to the contrary, it is to make even this worldliness dissolve.[3]

This theological view asserts that there is nothing that is not created by God and sustained by participation with God, and to establish a sovereign zone for anything requires rejecting participation and embracing nihilism. The consequences of this rejec-

2. In their introduction to *Radical Orthodoxy* they write that "the logic of secularism is imploding . . . it proclaims—uneasily, or else increasingly unashamedly—its own lack of values and lack of meaning. In its cyberspaces and theme-parks it promotes a materialism which is soulless, aggressive, nonchalant and nihilistic." *Radical Orthodoxy: A New Theology*, edited by John Milbank, Catherine Pickstock, and Graham Ward (London: Routledge, 1999) 1.

3. *Radical Orthodoxy: A New Theology*, 3.

tion for art are accordingly dismal: aesthetic experience is either reduced to an experience of brute materiality or sublimated into a purely intellectual sphere.

Of course, it is possible for art and aesthetics to get along without theology but only as *divertimenti* to distract us from the desert wastes we wander. To flourish, it must submit to being resituated within theology.

THEOLOGICAL CRITIQUE
OF THE KANTIAN SUBLIME

For Milbank and company the first step in resituating art and aesthetics within theology is a strong critique of the aesthetics of Kant. Particularly problematic is Kant's account of the sublime, which has been embraced as the aesthetic experience *non plus ultra*, enabling art and aesthetics to situate itself outside theology, resulting in the dire circumstance just noted. Their key criticism is that Kant's aesthetics of the sublime limits the sublime to an inter-subjective drama, precluding the revelation of a transcendent reality. For example:

> [T]he sublime is not to be sought in the things of nature, but only in our ideas . . . Nothing, therefore, which can be an object of the sense can be called sublime. But because there is in our imagination a striving toward infinite progress and in our reason a claim for absolute totality, regarded as a real idea, therefore this very inadequateness for that idea in our faculty for estimating the magnitude of things of sense excites in us the feeling of a supersensible faculty. And it is not the object of sense, but the use which the judgment naturally makes of certain objects on behalf of this latter feeling that is absolutely great, and in comparison every other use is small. Consequently it is the state of mind produced by a certain representation with which the reflective judgment is occupied, and not the object, that is to be called sublime . . . *the sublime is*

> *that, the mere ability to think which shows a faculty of the*
> *mind surpassing every standard of sense.*[4]

As this passage from the Third Critique shows, Kant's sublime is the subject's ability to overcome aesthetic awe. The subject emerges from the experience of the sublime enhanced, effectively reducing the sublime—the highest possibility for aesthetic experience and perhaps for conscious human experience—to a means to the end of aggrandizing the subject. What is "absolutely great" is not something outside the subject, but the human subject itself. As eminent philosopher Simon Blackburn humorously explains:

> In Kant's aesthetic theory the sublime "raises the soul above the height of vulgar commonplace." We experience the vast spectacles of nature as "absolutely great" and of irresistible might and power. This perception is fearful, but by conquering this fear and by regarding as small "those things of which we are wont to be solicitous" we quicken our sense of moral freedom. So we turn the experience of frailty and impotence into one of our true, inward moral freedom as the mind triumphs over nature and it is this triumph of reason that is truly sublime. Kant thus paradoxically places our sense of the sublime in an awareness of ourselves as transcending nature, rather than an awareness of ourselves as frail and insignificant. Most mountaineers and sailors disagree.[5]

Likewise theologians. Blackburn points out exactly the point of divergence between the Kantian sublime and the theological worldview: The former leaves the subject in control, with her powers of reason augmented by the "terrifying" experience of the sublime; in the latter, the experience of the transcendent is one in which the subject finds himself profoundly (to his *foundation*) interrupted.[6] As a professor of mine used to say, the difference

4. Immanuel Kant, *The Critique of Judgment*, sections 25, 28.

5. Simon Blackburn, *The Oxford Dictionary of Philosophy* (Oxford: Oxford University Press, 1996) 366.

6. One finds something of this sense in Edmund Burke's account of the sublime. Burke opens Part Two of *A Philosophical Enquiry into the Origin of*

is between something happening *in* your world and something happening *to* your world. The Kantian sublime lacks the power to alter the subject's world. It never presents the subject with something that it cannot, by dint of its newly enhanced faculties, assimilate to its extant understanding of the world. The sublime never presents the subject with something it cannot handle.

It troubles the Radical Orthodoxy school that here, at the pinnacle of modern and postmodern aesthetic experience, one does not find the subject trembling before a revelation of the transcendent reality of God. Instead, the subject self-centeredly trembles at the thought of his own annihilation, a trembling that is soon overcome via the mitigating offices of reason, leaving the subject less likely than ever to tremble before anything. Like an inoculation, Kant's sublime helps the subject resist future attacks of sublimity. In fine, Kant makes the sublime internal whereas for theologians the sublime is a revelation of a God who is transcendent and this irreducible to our internal states.

---

our Ideas of the Sublime and Beautiful with an analysis of astonishment, the "passion caused by the sublime." He writes. "[A]stonishment is that state of the soul, in which all its motions are suspended, with some degree of horror. In this case the mind is so entirely filled with its object, that it cannot entertain any other, nor by consequence reason on that object which employs it. Hence arises the great power of the sublime, that far from being produced by them, it anticipates our reasonings, and hurries us on by an irresistible force." See Edmund Burke, *A Philosophical Enquiry into the Origin of Our Ideas of the Sublime and Beautiful*, Boulton, ed. (Notre Dame, IN: University of Notre Dame Press, 1968) 57. This aspect of being overwhelmed by an irresistible force is precisely what is missing from Kant's account. For Kant the sublime has the effect of putting the subject in touch with its own freedom in the face of an overwhelming experience, and draws from the experience an aggrandized subject, more assured of its powers of reason and its moral freedom. In short, for Kant, in the face of the sublime reason has the last word, whereas for Burke, the sublime has the last word. For more on this crucial difference, see Jerome A. Miller *In The Throe of Wonder: Intimations of the Sacred in the Postmodern World* (Albany: SUNY Press, 1992). Miller connects the existential and phenomenological with the epistemological as he explores, among other things, this crucial difference between Burke and Kant. This work heavily influences my approach here.

THEOLOGICAL AESTHETICS

The criticism of Kant's aesthetics of the sublime is but a first, and alone inadequate, step. To paraphrase Thomas Merton, it is not enough to leave Egypt; one must also journey towards the Promised Land. The Radical Orthodoxy movement was conceived in part to rebut the thought of secular postmodernity but also as a corrective to those theologies which have cashiered their distinctiveness in order to accept it. Perhaps as a result of an extremely generous *mea culpa* acknowledging theology's occasional intolerance towards the secular, certain theologies have bent over backwards to accommodate secular thought to the extent that, in the view of the Radical Orthodoxy movement and others, they collapsed into it under the weight of their accommodations.[7]

Theology must forgo such accommodations if it is to entertain any hope of reclaiming the world ravaged by secular postmodern thought. In order to counter postmodern secularism and challenge the Kantian sublime, theology must recover and assert its distinctiveness *as* an alternative aesthetics. As Philip Blond, a contributor to *Radical Orthodoxy*, argues:

7. In the realm of aesthetics, they became unable to distinguish the Kantian sublime from the theological sublime. In F. C. Bauerschmidt's essay in *Radical Orthodoxy* the theological sublime, for Christians at least, is encountered in the form of Jesus Christ, a sign of frailty and insignificance, encountered uniquely in the Biblical narrative. Jesus is a sign, "*sous rature*; his whole life is one of negation of himself so as to be a sign that is transparent to the will of the Father … a sacrament of the God who is beyond human representation" (210). In this case, the experience of the sublime does not exalt the subject but reveals to him that he is transcended. As a sign "under erasure" it is constantly in the flux of the self-presentation of the un-representable God and thus is not readily available to theoretical apprehension nor is it surmountable by enhanced intellectual faculties. It is more like trying to grasp a slippery bar of soap. Precisely what makes the proverbial slippery bar of soap what it is, is its very eluding of the grasp that would handle it and keep it from slipping away. Neither the suspicious modern subject nor the postmodern scion provide an adequate understanding of the posture of the subject before the theological sublime, as they are both reliant on the will-to-power towards total and absolute realization of the free will. See Frederick Christian Bauerschmidt, "Aesthetics: The Theological Sublime," *Radical Orthodoxy: A New Theology*, 201–18.

> Theology has to recover its object, discern its own sensorium and locate this dimension of objectivity in the world so that all might see it. Does not St. Paul call for a new faculty of perception, for a subjectivity *not blinded by its own potency* . . . since "God however invisible has been there for the mind to see in the things he has made" (Rom. 1:20). This is a call for a recovery of perceptual ability, a theological aesthetics . . . if there are then theological modes of perception, might there also be a theological dimension to objects, present there for all to see?[8]

In theological circles, the mention of the recovery of theology's object and theological aesthetics immediately brings to mind the Swiss theologian Hans Urs Von Balthasar. His magisterial seven-volume *The Glory of The Lord* laid out a theological aesthetics as a corrective to a modern aesthetics that forsook the vision of the Glory of God, and it is the seam that Milbank, Blond and others work when they seek to develop a theological aesthetics.

For Balthasar, we have suffered a diminishment of aesthetic capacity with the emergence of modern thought. This correlates with the decline of *analogia entis*, the doctrine that states that the world participates in the divine reality of God. Volumes 4 and 5 of *The Glory of the Lord* characterize this moment as, notes one commentator, the decline of a poetic age and the beginning of a prosaic age.[9]

In his diagnosis, Balthasar followed the work of Jesuit Erich Przywara[10] whose import Balthasar scholar Edward Oakes summarizes thus:

8. Philip Blond, *Post-Secular Philosophy: Between Philosophy and Theology* (London: Routledge, 1998) 4.

9. Edward T. Oakes, *Pattern of Redemption* (New York, Contiuuum, 2004).

10. In his two-part essay "Beyond the Sublime: The Aesthetics of the Analogy of Being" John R. Betz examines in detail Balthasar's defense of Przywara against Karl Barth's unrelenting critiques of his account of the doctrine of analogy. Barth, apparently, was determined to see in the doctrine of analogy an attempt to usurp the unique soteriological import of the revelation of Christ by predicating the redemptive relationship made possible by Christ upon an extant relationship of being. Barth felt that the doctrine of analogy made God

> According to Przywara, the history of modern thought may be interpreted as the inability to hold together the polarity between God's transcendence and immanence; that is, as running aground either in the pathos of stressing God's omnipotence, thereby robbing the world of its own reality by overwhelming it with God's transcendence, as in Luther, or by the world absorbing God into itself through a pantheistic identification with him, as in Spinoza . . . the whole of philosophy was the story of this unfulfilled passion for wholeness. [Przywara] could see how *all* philosophy was continually running aground, both because of the almost inevitable failure of every individual person to harness the tensions in the human soul and because those tensions are but the psychological reflection of the inner structure of the universe's relation to God.[11]

and humanity too similar in such a way that the grace of God could be considered to inhere in humanity by virtue or their analogical participation in God's being. But, as Przywara points out, "*analogia entis* signifies that what is decisive in "every similarity, however great," is the "ever greater dissimilarity." Betz, *Modern Theology* 22 (January 10, 2006). Perhaps Jean-Luc Marion's critique of an ontological notion of transubstantiation helps here. He rejects the understanding of transubstantiation as the mere conversion from one kind of being to another, a movement that takes place wholly within the ontological realm, because this fails to consider a God beyond being. A God who is beyond being participating in being has radical implications for ontology. The Eucharist, in part, is the revelation of this possibility within being, a revelation that promises to alter the being within which it is revealed. Doctrinal obsessions with the status of the matter involved (bread, body) limit the sacramental to the ontological, telling only half of the story. The sacrament, like the person of Christ who hypostatically unifies the divine and the human, heaven and earth, illuminates within being being's origin beyond being, and thus its contingency as being and its intrinsic nothingness. Certain doctrinal arguments about transubstantiation seek to install God within being precisely to rid being of its inherent contingency. By collapsing Creator into creation the latter seems no longer contingent. Naturalizing the supernatural, to borrow a phrase from Milbank, is a way of recoiling from contingency. It implicitly rejects the analogical sense and eventuates in materialism; a glorified materialism, but materialism nonetheless. See *God Without Being*, trans. Thomas Carlson (Chicago: University of Chicago Press, 1995).

11. Oakes, *Pattern of Redemption*, 36.

Przywara saw the restoration of the doctrine of analogy as a means of "breaking through the closed horizon of modern consciousness and its nearly exclusive concern with either the world or man-in-the-world."[12]

Theology, too, became prosaic, closed horizon-ed, to the extent that it embraced these aspects of modern thought and turned its back on the doctrine of analogy. For Balthasar, "Christian thinking [has been impoverished] by the growing loss of this perspective which once so strongly informed theology," and stands in need of restoration. To this end, Balthasar recommends that theology reconnect with it estranged aesthetic self: "It is not... our intent to yield to some whim and force theology into a little traveled side-road, but rather to restore theology to a main artery which it has abandoned."[13] To return to itself, theology must embrace the aesthetic.

Why is aesthetics the royal road to restoring theology? As it modernized, theology became increasingly fixated on questions of ethics and epistemology, amenable to concerns for the world or man-in-the-world, leaving aesthetics behind. These are integral for theology, but without a similar concern for the aesthetic, theology would lose much of what distinguishes it from philosophy, a largely secular discourse that also speaks to these concerns. Balthasar explains: "Why is [his theological aesthetics] called *The Glory of the Lord*? Because it is concerned, first, with learning to see God's revelation and because God can be known only in his Lordliness . . . which the NT calls *gloria*. This means that God does not come primarily as a teacher for the true, but to display and to radiate the splendor of [God's] true love and true beauty. *Aisthesis*, the act of perception, and *Aistheton*, the particular thing perceived . . . together inform the object of theology."[14]

12. Oakes, *Pattern of Redemption*, 40.

13. Hans Urs von Balthasar, *The Glory of the Lord: A Theological Aesthetics: Volume 1: Seeing the Form* (London: T. & T. Clark, 2001).

14. Hans Urs von Balthasar, *The Glory of the Lord: A Theological Aesthetics: Volume 2: Clerical Styles* (London: T. & T. Clark, 2001) 213.

Balthasar did not wish to over-correct and grant the aesthetic primacy of place. Theology cannot sustain itself on the vision of beauty alone, neglecting truth and goodness, though to forsake it desperately attenuates theological accounts of truth and goodness. [15] Theologically speaking, beauty, truth and goodness are all part of God, but of these three it is the aesthetic aspect of God, *gloria*, that especially displays analogical tension.

BEAUTY'S SACRAMENTAL SWAY

Balthasar finds the analogical tension necessary to restore theology uniquely evident in the experience of beauty, particularly in beauty's ability to captivate. The experience of being aesthetically captivated critically differentiates it from other aesthetic experiences. Indeed, it might be more appropriate to speak of it in terms of a captivating aesthetic *encounter*, since the language of experience seems tied to the Kantian aesthetics we are trying to surpass. [16] To explain: A subject has an experience of an object. In an experience, the subject does all the experiencing while the

15. These stakes are high for Balthasar because they are for Thomas Aquinas, progenitor of the doctrine of analogy. How high is made very clear by Milbank and Pickstock in *Truth in Aquinas* (London: Routledge, 2001). They see that Beauty is indispensable to knowledge: "[I]nsofar as Beauty is involved in the manifestation of things in their integrity, without which there could be no visibility, it is fundamental to knowledge . . . and insofar as Beauty is linked with desire, it is crucial to the outgoings or ecstases of the will and the Good." They continue: "Thus Beauty shows Goodness through itself and the Good leads to the true, yet we could never look at these relations as at a measurable distance. And this sense of something immanently disclosed through something else in an unmeasurable way, but in a fashion experienced as harmonious, is precisely something *aesthetic*. Every judgment of truth for Aquinas is an aesthetic judgment." An experience of *aesthesis*, a moment of beholding/being beholden to someone/something that calls me to attend it and compels me to inquire into it, is the beginning of knowledge. Knowledge is, contra modern epistemological portraits of it, not something that proceeds from the ego by dint of intention, but rather is spurred—perhaps irresistibly—in the moment of *aesthesis*.

16. For more on this difference, consult the works of Emmanuel Levinas and Jean-Luc Marion.

object remains inert. Think of experience as a one-way street where the subject's consciousness freely moves past the object. In an encounter, as the word implies, the subject is met with and countered by something irreducible to an object of experience. Countered, the subject's free movement is inhibited. The beauty Balthasar describes is encountered beauty.

So, what is it about the *encounter* with beauty that is so decisive?[17] By way of further explanation, consider this story about Donatello from Vasari's *Lives of the Artists*: "Walking home one day from market with an apronful of eggs, the sculptor Donatello happened to pass by the door of the chapel in which the newly finished crucifix of Brunelleschi had just been hung. He was so stricken by the beauty of what he saw that he dropped all his eggs and stood there transfixed."[18]

Whence comes beauty's sway? What does it mean to be *stricken* and *transfixed* by beauty? Of the myriad objects in his purview, why did the beauty of Brunelleschi's crucifix claim Donatello's attention in such a way that nothing else claimed his attention at all, not even the immediate task of safely transporting

17. Oakes offers: "Recall why hearing has primacy: you cannot listen away—it has the least control over what it perceives and because what it hears is merely the self-communicating word that the other wishes to impart. And so hearing expresses the obediential moment of faith more than any other perceptive faculty. *Hearing hands over control to the other*, all the while *receiving* what the other wishes to communicate. Vision, however, as we have seen, has things more under control . . . except in one case . . . beauty. If the stance of hearing is fundamentally one of assent, so too may we say the same of the inherent response to beauty: 'Is not our every encounter with the beautiful,' says Balthasar quoting the protestant Gerhard Nebel, 'tantamount to an assent to creation, either bestowed on us or drawn from us?' . . . This remark. . . . captures . . . why [Balthasar] places aesthetics as the starting point of his theology: for it is an analysis of the nature of beauty that we see how sight and hearing can be fused into one total of assent to God's gifts of creation and revelation. For what beauty proves is that sight is not in as much control as it might first assume. Beauty by its very nature always elicits a response: one cannot simply experience a form or phenomenon as beautiful without responding, without *assenting.*" Oakes, *Pattern of Redemption,* 41.

18. Taken from Vasari's *The Lives of the Artists.* Though this is Vasari's story, it is here retold by J. Miller in *In the Throe of Wonder.*

his eggs? Seemingly, the world in which the task of carrying eggs was important came to a sudden end as, stricken and transfixed, Donatello became unreservedly attentive to the beauty that stood before him in the crucifix. Yet, how could an experience of seeing *beauty* so intrude upon his familiar world so as to suspend his engagement in that world? Seeing beauty, Donatello encounters a reality that overthrows the reality familiar to him.

At the heart of the experience of the beautiful as revelation of transcendent reality is the realization that one has been exposed to a reality beyond one's self. But how do we recognize this reality as greater than our own unless it is somehow understandable in terms of our own? Indeed, it would seem that if this reality could be construed in terms of our reality then it would somehow be reducible to our extant categories of experience; therefore it would not be the experience of a reality beyond our own, but merely a super-experience of our familiar reality (*à la* Kantian sublime). But this assumes that such a reality can only be rendered according to our extant knowledge of this reality; that it isn't perceptible without our bringing categories of knowing to bear on it. What of the possibility that the perception of such a reality *does not* rely upon our extant categories of experiencing and knowing, because the ability to perceive such a reality *is revealed simultaneously with the revelation of that reality*?

In contrast to locating beauty in the eye of the beholder, where the appearance of beauty is the result of a correspondence between the subject's idea of beauty and what the subject perceives as fitting that idea, the encounter with beauty is rather a case of the subject *being seen by* beauty.[19] It is beauty's gaze that transfixes the subject, seemingly choosing her rather than her choosing it, and transforms her in so doing.[20] It is with this in

---

19. Or, as William Desmond puts it, "to behold is to be *beholden* to." Cf. *Being and the Between.*

20. I try to demonstrate this to students—and it is a brute method, I admit—by asking them if they *chose* to find the sunrise *beautiful* or were they rather *surprised* by the sunrise's beauty. Being smitten by the beautiful is unexpected, unlooked-for.

mind that Balthasar recalls the closing lines of Rilke's *Archaic Torso of Apollo*: "There is no place in it which does not see you. You must change your life." The life-change implicit in this transformation of seeing is nothing less than the transformation of one's entire way of being. For Balthasar, writes John Riches, "It is the perception of beauty which creates a dimension between the ground and its appearing which opens our eyes to a perception of being, to a perception of an objective reality set over against the beholder which is lovely and desirable."[21] As one's vision is transformed so also is one's reality.

It is precisely one of the qualities of beauty, the same quality that makes it an encounter rather than an experience, to outstrip our perception of it. Beauty floods the perception of it and to perceive it is, perhaps unwittingly, to *partake of* its reality. One cannot measure this partaking. Imagine trying to sip a flood. One is rather caught up in the flood, carried away by it. In partaking one is, in a sense, taken. Beauty has a sacramental character, and seeing it can be called *sacramental vision.*

What makes a sacrament and what makes it transformative? This can be answered perhaps most concisely by marking the distinction between sacrament and sign. Simply understood, a sign indicates something else. For example, a STOP sign has no meaning in itself, but indicates or delivers a meaning, and is then disposable once that meaning is delivered.[22] A sacrament is not an indicator, disposable once the meaning has been shucked from it, but rather *is* the thing it points to. Theologically speaking, the sacrament does not merely indicate transcendence, but *is* the advent of a new reality shot through with the transcendent. Through the sacrament the transcendent comes to dwell in immanence and, dwelling there, alters it. No longer is immanence merely immanence, but now it is a sacramental reality. Reality is radically transformed as it becomes a sacrament.

21. John Riches, *The Analogy of Beauty: The Theology of Hans Urs von Balthasar* (London: T. & T. Clark, 1986) 50–51.

22. Robert Hughes, *The Shock of the New* (New York: McGraw-Hill, 1990).

And so, beauty's sacramental character is analogical. The sacrament maintains the analogical tension between transcendence and immanence so important to Balthasar and offers an alternative account of beauty that neither collapses it into the realm of brute materiality nor sublimates it to the realm of pure intellect. The sacrament transforms vision and keeps it open to the unfolding richness of revelation and open to continual transformation.

A POSTMODERN DEMUR

Theological aesthetics' compelling critique of modern and postmodern aesthetics makes clear that the transcendent must be honored as such if contemporary religious art wishes to eschew its predecessors' failings. A sacramental vision guards against both idealism and materialism and keeps the world, the field of aesthetic experience and the very elements of every artwork, far richer than either can render it. It seems as though the routing of the Kantian sublime and the transformation of perception through sacramental vision could give rise to a new religious art that would give theologians little reason to demur. Yet, there are those who for any number of reasons remain outside theological discourses, though they might concur about the limitations of Kant's aesthetics and the shortcomings of idealism and materialism. From these, we can imagine a demur before departing the postmodern desert.

For contemporary art to acknowledge the difference between the Kantian sublime and the revelation of the transcendent would not amount to adopting the theological framework of Milbank and Balthasar. Their critiques of Kant's aesthetics might persuade contemporary art that it must open itself to a discourse beyond itself, possibly theological, if it does not wish to persist in the isolating autonomy that is partly to blame for the estrangement of art and theology.

But can postmodern selves who are suspicious of theological talk of revelation and transcendent realities, and who have long since cast off such superstitious stuff have an aesthetic religious experience? Even if they encountered in beauty the Glory of the Lord, would they acknowledge it as such? How would the postmodern subject—with nothing but the language of the Kantian sublime in which to articulate this experience—express this experience if not in the language of the Kantian sublime?

To those who do not share the theological tradition we have been examining here, the cultivation of sacramental vision as a remedy to the materialism and nihilism of postmodernity might seem unattainable. Which points to a more critical question: Is sacramental vision impossible *ex ecclesia*? Is it possible to sincerely attend the manifestation of transcendence, at least provisionally, situated outside a theological framework in the desert of postmodernity?

If contemporary art cannot or does not find itself resituated within a theological framework, what is it to do?

FOUND SACRAMENTS IN THE DESERT

As Catholic philosopher Josef Pieper suggested, art *qua* art holds the potential to transform vision *à la* sacramental vision:

> Before you can express anything in tangible form, you first need eyes to see. The mere attempt, therefore, to create an artistic form compels the artist to take a fresh look at the visible reality; it requires *authentic and personal* observation. Long before a creation is completed, the artist has gained . . . another and more *intimate* achievement: a deeper and *more receptive* vision, a more intense awareness, a sharper more discerning understanding, a more *patient openness*…an eye for things previously overlooked. In short: the artist will be able to perceive with new eyes the abundant wealth of all visible reality, and, thus challenged additionally acquires the inner capacity to absorb into his mind such an exceedingly rich harvest. The capacity to *see* increases.[23]

23. Joseph Pieper, *Learning To See Again*, in *Only the Lover Sings: Art and Contemplation* (Fort Collins, CO: Ignatius, 1990) 34.

Art is quasi-sacramental at its heart, developing an alternate vision of the ordinary and sharing it with us, so that our vision might be transformed. The vision native to art and sacramental vision are kindred, however estranged they may have become. This is a basic assertion of a theological aesthetics: theology and art are sisters, both handmaidens to the revelation of transcendence.

In light of this kinship something like a found sacrament appears possible. "Everything conceivable," asserts Colleen McDannell in *Material Christianity*, "can be a sacred object." Theological aesthetics couldn't have put it better itself. Remaining receptive in patient openness to such potential inhering in *everything* is a posture that can be adopted from theological aesthetics without first imbibing explicitly theological tenets. Here we should note well that one of the most fundamental assertions theologians make about God is that God is God with or without theology,[24] a humbling assertion which keeps theologians chary about restricting the field of potentially revelatory objects to those that meet their approval. The revelation of transcendence bloweth wither it listeth.

From the perspective of a theological aesthetics grounded in the doctrine of analogy, it seems that anything in the realm of the aesthetic could already be on the verge of the theological and vice versa, and in this way *all* aesthetic phenomena are theologically relevant. Moreover, an aesthetics informed by sacramental vision should view any and every aesthetic object, even those that are the products of avowedly atheistic worldviews, as potentially revelatory of transcendence. Sacramental vision remains open to the possibility of revelation where one might otherwise least expect it and compels us to keep our eyes open when it does not appear.

---

24. Given what it is, theology's greatest achievements should be at the same time its most humbling moments. Consider Thomas Aquinas' famous opinion of his work towards the end of his life: "[A]ll that I have written seems like straw to me (*mihi videtur ut palea*)."

While resituating contemporary art within a theological framework has a certain appeal to those concerned that postmodernity's creeping nihilism will finally evacuate all meaning from art, the situation we find ourselves in while rethinking the relationship between art and theology is from within the postmodern desert. These questions concerning the relationship of these two handmaidens have to be posed and considered from within this desert. Yet, we may take heart: for the desert, while a place of wandering and despair, is also, as theologians who read their Bibles know, a locus of revelation.

4

In Excess: Jean-Luc Marion, Bill Viola, and the Theological Sublime

Ronald R. Bernier

In 1983, American artist, Bill Viola first exhibited the sound and video installation, *Room for St. John of the Cross*, a spatial, temporal and aural environment, comprised of a black box enclosure—approximately 6 x 5 x 5.5 feet—confined within a larger darkened room, itself measuring 14 x 24 x 30 feet; on one side of the black cubicle was a small window opening through which glowed a soft incandescent light. As viewers approached and peered through the small aperture into an otherwise inaccessible room of white walls and dirt floor—minimally furnished with a wooden table on which sat a pitcher, a glass of water, and a four-inch color video monitor—they could hear the barely audible incantation, in Spanish, of St. John's love poetry. The religious reformer composed this work between 1577 and 1578 while imprisoned for nine months in a space the same size as the cubicle and subjected, through daily torture, to what he called his "dark night of the soul." That "night" was a deep and profound sense of abandonment not only by his faith community, but by God himself. It was from these depths of abjection and solitude, however, that St. John composed this most passionate poetry, in which he speaks of the in-pouring of God into the soul, an experience of profound love and ecstasy. Outside the small cell, in Viola's re-staging, viewers are unsteadied by a large-screen quaking video projection, in black and white, of a snow-covered mountain range shot with an unstable hand-held camera, all of this accompanied by the unrelenting roar of wind and white noise saturating the room. Meanwhile, on the small video monitor inside the cell, a similar mountain view glows quietly and motionless in vivid color as natural light shifts in real space and time. At once, viewers are made to feel their own incarceration in the larger room, invited to imagine the imprisoned reformer and to contemplate the meaning of his (and our) suffering. As historian David Morgan has aptly put it: "Viola's installations bear the conviction that the conditions of traditional religious ritual can be simulated in works of art, in order to achieve something of the spiritual transformation wrought in the original context."[1] And a note published in 1982 while the artist was still at work on this piece, Viola confirmed: "Initiation rites and age-old spiritual training ordeals . . . are all controlled, staged accidents, ancient technologies designed to bring the organism to a life-threatening crises."[2]

This threatening crisis and its spiritual dimension, I shall argue, invoke the rich philosophical tradition of the aesthetic *sublime*, and more specifically its basic duality of pain and pleasure. Viola's art investigates our human condition as embodied beings, and urges us toward the performance of vulnerability, yearning but ill-equipped for transcendence and the ultimate renunciation of Self, and does so via the ancient traditions of Christian mysticism and, more specifically, via *apophatic*, or negative, theology—the idea that God (or the divine) is best identified in terms of "absence," "otherness," and "difference;" this, ultimately, will have resonance in contemporary notions of negation as developed in continental philosophy and in particular in postmodern deconstructive critiques of Enlightenment ideals.

1. Chris Townsend, ed., *The Art of Bill Viola* (London: Thames & Hudson, 2004) 105.

2. Ibid.

VIOLA ON CHRISTIAN MYSTICISM

In a 1997 interview, Viola remarked on his discoveries of the figures of Early Christianity, and the sixteenth-century mystics John of the Cross and his mentor Teresa of Avila, as well as the earlier fourteenth-century Dominican German cleric Meister Eckhart, and the anonymous author of the medieval text, *The Cloud of Unknowing*, all within the Christian tradition of the *via negativa*:

> The *via negativa* in the West is connected to a shadowy fifth-century character known as Pseudo-Dionysius the Aeropagite, who … described an immanent God, the deity that is within each person (an Eastern concept), as opposed to the transcendent God of the more familiar *via positiva*, over and above all and outside the individual. The *via positiva* describes God as the ultimate expression of a series of attributes or qualities—good, all-seeing, all-knowing, etc.—of which human beings contain lesser, diminished versions … The *via negativa*, on the other hand, is the way of negation. God is wholly other and cannot be described or comprehended. There are no attributes other than unknowability. When the mind faces the divine reality, it seizes up and enters a "cloud of unknowing," or to use St. John of the Cross' term, "a dark night of the soul." Here in the darkness, the only thing to go on is faith, and the only way to approach God is from within, primarily through love. This is why much of St. John's poetry reads like classic love poems.[3]

Here Viola draws an important connection, as he sees it, between the sixteenth-century saints John of the Cross and Teresa of Avila and their medieval mystic forebears, tracing the history back even to Pseudo-Dionysius the Areopagite in the fifth century and, specifically, to *apophatic theology*—that is, to efforts to speak of God only in terms of what may *not* be said about God, a "negative theology" allied with the approaches of mysticism.

3. *Bill Viola*, exhibition catalogue (New York: Whitney Museum of American Art, 1998) 144.

Negative theology is a tradition the sources for which are found in late antiquity and the early Christian period, reaching its first significant high point in the Neoplatonic philosophy of the third century AD, with yet more radical representations found among the mystics of the late Middle Ages.[4] This tradition is fostered by a fundamental notion essentially opposed to the central tenet of classical Greek philosophy of Being (or ontology) and its claims for autonomous human reason; rather, what human desire truly seeks—the divine—cannot be defined, pronounced, or known because it is radically transcendent, incommensurably *other*, beyond the subject and outside the limit of rationality and the hubris of classical philosophy. Negative theology's emphasis on the unknowableness and the unutterableness of the divine informs the notion that "transcendence is best approached via denials, via what according to earthly concepts *is not*."[5] Thus, for St. John of the Cross, abandonment, silence, and the experience of divine *absence* is understood to be the veiled *presence* of divine fullness—for in hiddenness is revelation.[6]

In language, this deliberate refusal of clarity, Denys Turner argues, is precisely what appeals in medieval mysticism to postmodern thought, with its "messages of the decentering and fragmentation of knowledge, of the collapse of stable relations between cognitive subjects and the objects of their knowledge, of the destablizations of fixed relations between signifier and signified."[7] We will have occasion, later in this essay, to assess this view of the inadequacy of language seemingly shared between apophatic theology and postmodern deconstructors, and, more specifically, to mark the crucial distinctions between them—and,

4. Ilse N. Bulhof and Laurens ten Kate, eds., *Flight of the Gods: Philosophical Perspectives on Negative Theology* (New York: Fordham University Press, 2000) 4–5.

5. Ibid., 5.

6. See also in this context Oliver Davies and Denys Turner, eds., *Silence and the Word: Negative Theology and Incarnation* (Cambridge: Cambridge University Press, 2002).

7. Denys Turner, "The Art of Unknowing: Negative Theology in Late Medieval Mysticism," *Modern Theology* 14 (1998) 473.

indeed, where Viola aligns himself. But first, it is important to draw a closer connection between John of the Cross, his own Reformation context, and the traces of such in Viola's 1983 installation.

ST. JOHN OF THE CROSS AND MYSTIC FOREBEARS

As a founder, along with Teresa of Avila, of the reformist order the Discalced Carmelites, John of the Cross was imprisoned in Toledo by his superiors in December of 1577 for his refusal to desist in efforts to reform the Carmelite order.[8] Incarcerated for nine months, he was subjected to regular torture and public floggings, managing to escape in August of 1578, during which time, in seeking relief, he composed the greater part of his poem *Spiritual Canticle*, a symbolic variation on the *Song of Songs* which narrates the nighttime journey of a bride (the human soul) as she searches for her lost lover (Christ). The Bride's "dark night of the soul"—giving the title to St. John's second major piece—narrates the hardships and difficulties she endures in her progressive detachment from the world toward reaching the light of union with her lover; it is a painful experience of spiritual maturation, through loss and then transformation of the self, toward ultimate union with God. And just as in darkness there is privation of light, this journey demands privation and purgative suffering. Finally, in the *Ascent of Mount Carmel* and its account of the soul's ascetical search for perfect union, St. John chronicles the ineffable and unutterable mystical experiences along the way toward ecstatic encounter with the Divine experienced in contemplation.

In apophatic or negative theology it is in these terms that the Divine is ineffable, an abstract experience that can only be recognized or experienced —that is, human beings cannot describe the essence of God, and therefore all descriptions, if attempted will be by necessity false. Neither existence *nor* nonexistence as we understand it applies to God; in this sense, God is beyond

8. See Kieran Kavanaugh and Otilio Rodriguez, eds. and trans., *The Collected Works of St. John of the Cross* (Washington, DC: ICS, 1991) *passim*.

existing or, as contemporary phenomenologist Jean-Luc Marion will have it, "God without Being." In other words, God is not a creation, not conceptually definable in terms of space and location, and not conceptually confinable to assumptions of temporality. This, as I've suggested, is not unrelated to the philosophical and aesthetic traditions of the *sublime,* which similarly seeks to transcend language and its conceptual categories no longer adequate to their expressive or descriptive tasks.

Much of Bill Viola's work is precisely about that cultivation of individual experience of ineffable divine reality as beyond the realm or limits of ordinary perception. In an interview published in 1993, the artist sounds a familiar note:

> The basic tenets of the Via Negativa are the unknowability of God: that God is wholly other, independent, complete; that God cannot be grasped by the human intellect, cannot be described in any way; that when the mind faces the divine reality, it becomes blank. It seizes up. It enters a cloud of unknowing. When the eyes cannot see, then the only thing to go on is faith, and the only true way to approach God is from within. From that point the only way God can be reached is though love. By love the soul enters into union with God, a union not infrequently described through the metaphor of ecstatic sex.[9]

Here, and in the later 1997 interview cited above, Viola makes direct and repeated reference to Pseudo-Dionysius the Areopagite, the anonymous theologian and philosopher of the late 5th to early 6th century whose works were ascribed to Dionysius the Areopagite, the Athenian convert of St. Paul mentioned in Acts 17.

In Dionysius' *De Divinus Nominibus* (*The Divine Names*)—a text with strong Neoplatonic influence that grew to be immensely popular amongst medieval theologians—beauty is identified as an attribute of God and inseparably conjoined with the Good. It is an idea based on Plato's notion, set out in the *Timaeus,* that the

---

9. Quoted in Townsend, *The Art of Bill Viola,* 131.

world is the product of a rational, purposive design, and that it is meant to be a good environment for human beings and non-human entities, which have themselves been deliberately produced (created) by that greater intelligence that designed the world. Plato's *Timaeus* concludes: "For with this our world has received its full complement of living creatures, mortal and immortal, and come to be in all its grandeur, goodness, beauty and perfection—this visible living creature made in the likeness of the intelligible and embracing all the visible, this god displayed to sense, this our heaven, one and only-begotten."[10] This classical vision of the cosmos was then translated in the medieval world into emphatically Christian terms, via the doctrine of analogy or *analogia entis*. Relying on Plato's distinction between physical and (unknowable) ultimate reality, Pseudo-Dionysius treated material reality as an emanation from Absolute Being, or Absolute Beauty, which transcends the whole of sensible nature but remains continuous with it in the sense of what emanates from it. All created things on this view are theophanies or manifestations of God; the world participates in the divine reality of God. Thus, the Good and the Beautiful are taken to be one and the same and both have their identity in God. So, in experiencing that which is beautiful in this world, we are experiencing the "anagogical" or upward moving of the mind from the world of appearances to a contemplation of divine love. And this systematic analogy-making was a way of knowing the world; it involved both the philosophical habit of seeing the hand of God in the beauty of the world—a symbolism for the mind which perceived relations obtaining between the phenomenologies of the physical and the metaphysical—and the more conventional perception of the world as a divine work of art, such that everything in it possessed allegorical (and thus moral), in addition to literal, meanings, as if the world were designed to be interpreted for those meanings.

10. Plato, *Timaeus*, quoted in Umberto Eco, *Art and Beauty in the Middle Ages* (New Haven: Yale University Press, 1986) 17.

Yet, the Pseudo-Dionysius further argues, divine "names" such as Beauty, Goodness, Love, Wisdom, or even Being, can be applied to God only *analogically* and therefore, in the end, inadequately; these names are both like and unlike human goodness, beauty, wisdom or being. For Dionysius, these names can be applied to God affirmatively (that is, cataphatically)—God is of course a good, wise, beautiful and loving being—but their inadequacy is at once realized for their deficiency and this recognition leads to apophaticism (or the erasure or crossing out of these terms). God is *not* good or wise or beautiful or loving or powerful in the way we, as humans, understand these qualities or terms. The closer we come to naming the reality that is God, the more the inadequacy and impotence of our ordinary language is in evidence. "If talk about God is deficient," Denys Turner argues, "this is a discovery made within the extending of it into superfluity, into that excess in which it collapses under its own weight . . . [T]he silence which falls in the embarrassment of prolixity is transformed into awe."[11] Negative theology, then, *affirms* a not-knowing, a silence; it is a "language of unsaying."[12] Silence, or the refusal of discursive reflection, is a form of communication, wherein something is known at the somatic level. This denial of all namable divine essentiality will be central to Jean-Luc Marion's thinking, and to our sense of a theological aesthetics in Viola's work, founded on an analogy between aesthetic experience and that of revelation—a new sense of Beauty that reveals something beyond our experience and unites us to that revelation, or intimation of the sublime beneath the visible surface of observable phenomena.

THE CLOUD OF UNKNOWING

Another of the medieval mystics consistently invoked by Viola is the anonymous author of *The Cloud of Unknowing*, a practical

11. Davies and Turner, *Silence and the Word*, 18.
12. Ibid., 23.

spiritual guidebook believed to have been written in the latter half of the fourteenth century by an anonymous English monk who counsels a young student to seek God not through knowledge but through affectivity, what he calls a "naked blind feeling of being." The author urges his disciple to negate all cognitive activity, an active effort of denial and unknowing, which allows for the irruption of grace into the ordinary.[13] Cheryl Taylor has compellingly theorized this notion of transcendence within the context of *liminality*, a condition of open-ended betweenness—that is, between the traditional dualism of the active and contemplative lives, a space of "potential."[14] In this way the subject, rendered "naked," vulnerable, is stripped of the familiar, of the stable and the normative, and is placed in a transitional or liminal space, challenged and thus transformed by the very impress of the unfamiliar. In this fissured subjectivity the subject is a *self-in-process*, open to the functioning of grace within the soul.[15] The *Cloud* Author says of this process: "For when you first begin to undertake it, all that you find is a darkness, a sort of cloud of unknowing . . . This darkness and cloud is always between you and your God . . . and it prevents you from seeing him clearly by the light of understanding in your reason . . . When I say 'darkness,' I mean a privation of knowing."[16] This metaphor of darkness or obscurity converges with Scripture in the Exodus story of Moses' encoun-

13. See Denys Turner, *Darkness of God: Negativity in Christian Mysticism* (Cambridge: Cambridge University Press, 1995) chapter 8.

14. Cheryl Taylor, "The *Cloud* Texts and Some Aspects of Modern Theory," *Mystics Quarterly* 24/4 (2001). This sense of *transitus* in liminality is often invoked by Viola himself in the enigmatic titles of some of his pieces, e.g., *Crossing, Passing,* etc.

15. Maika J. Will draws a distinction of agency of grace—God or man—between the Pseudo-Dionysius and the *Cloud* Author: "the Areopagite suggests that the soul is given the grace to raise itself up to the transcendent God, while the *Cloud* author maintains instead that the transcendent God descends into the soul to work there directly through operant grace." Maika J. Will, "Dionysian Neoplatonism and the Theology of the Cloud Author—I," *Downside Review* (April 1992) 189; see also part two of this study, in the June 1992 issue.

16. *The Cloud of Unknowing*, foreword by Tim Farrington, ed. Emilie Griffin (Mahwah, NJ: HarperCollins, 1981) 10–11, 17.

ter with God "in a dark cloud" on Mount Sinai (Exodus 20:21). In these meanings, faith is the darkness of un/non-knowing, the stripping away of material elements that hamper apprehension of the divine. Dark knowledge is dark in the sense that it is not a conceptual knowledge. This process of privation or renunciation of the attachments of the self to its own operations and objects is dark because it removes from us our foundations of comfort and sources of fulfillment and transplants us into nothingness—this is the feeling of abandonment or powerlessness as St. John of the Cross described it.

The *Cloud of Unknowing,* with its central metaphors of negativity and hiddenness, draws on the mystical tradition of Pseudo-Dionysius which, as has been argued, has inspired generations of mystical searchers including St. John of the Cross. It draws also on the earlier, fourteen-century Dominican philosopher-preacher Meister Eckhart, whose mystical speculations are grounded in a linguistic strategy of opaqueness and paradox, and unusual metaphors and neologisms, in order to provoke unknowing through the very demonstration of language's inadequacies; Eckhart's is a language saturated with tropes of "nothingness," "emptiness," and "abyss," steeped in images of stepping outside the self.[17] According to Eckhart, we must abandon the picture we have of God. Every speaking, every image, every concept is insufficient. Human language and its conceptual apparatus are surpassed and affirm a not-knowing and a silence (a *not-* or *un-*saying). The absolute ineffability of God provides the motive for the bewildering way in which Eckhart speaks about divine nature.[18] His is a rhetoric designed to induce—through its refusal of stability, ultimacy and

---

17. Viola speaks about reading Eckhart's sermons during his own self-isolating retreats to read and write. See Whitney catalogue (1998) 145.

18. See *Meister Eckhart: The Essential Sermons, Commentaries, Treatises, and Defense,* translated and introduction by Edmund Colledge, OSA and Bernard McGinn (Mahwah, NJ: Paulist, 1981).

coherence—unknowing and the dispersal of meaning, a tendency not lost on Derrida and other postmodern theologies.[19]

Finally, this "deconstructive" activity in language in the end signals the disablement of the intellect in the same sense, I think, that makes operative and relevant the encounter with the *sublime*. Apophaticism simply shows, Denys Turner writes, "that God cannot be known intellectually. The clutter of intellect and language being cleared away, room is left in a darkness of the consequent *intellectual* unknowing; and there it is love which yields a direct experience of God unmediated by any work of thought or intellect."[20] But while the negative theologian and the deconstructivist share a similar interest in the ineffable—in that which escapes total description—mystical language and its imagery, I suggest, retain the *gesture* beyond themselves into the realm of unmediated wisdom in the sublime, the transcendental signified.[21] That is to say, there is *something* that is unsayable; we know from faith it is not a nothing. It is, in fact, as Derrida called it in *Languages of the Unsayable*, "the language of promise," or, perhaps better I would offer, a language of *hope*, situated in the midst of promise, of the *not-yet* or the *unfinished*, and with hope, trust and openness to infinite and overwhelming possibilities.

19. Eckhart's disorienting discourse has been characterized as Christianity with a Zen outlook, particularly its emphasis on the process of emptying the self of self-will in order to recognize that union with God already exists in the soul; this connection would not have been lost on Viola who early on turned to close study of Eastern enlightenment philosophy and spiritual engagement from Buddhism to the Persian Sufi mystic Rumi. In fact, Viola's *Room for St. John of the Cross* was recently reassembled for the exhibition at the Guggenheim Museum in New York, *The Third Mind: American Artists Contemplate Asia*. It is also worth noting here that even Edmund Burke's locating of the sublime in terrifying states of isolation and emptiness (discussed below), pointing towards a concept of the void, has its own resonance in Asian spirituality.

20. Turner, "Art of Unknowing," 484.

21. On the use of the term "transcendental signified," see Nike Kocijaneie Pokorn, "The Language and Discourse of the Cloud of Unknowing," *Literature & Theology* 11 (1997) 408–21.

KANT AND THE SUBLIME

All of this, then, is closely tied, on my reading, to philosophical and aesthetic theories of the sublime, in which the whole question of transcendence looms large. The sublime, for Kant, was that experience which reveals to the mind Nature's power to suggest to the imagination, to intimate and embody, what is visually unrepresentable. In the presence of the sublime—denoted, as Kant had it, by vast and powerful objects and overwhelming spaces—we are reminded that Nature as boundless manifold is not ours to know completely. This experience—what Kant called the *mathematical sublime* (in terms of vast size) and the *dynamical sublime* (great power, force and energy)—is such that our perceptual faculties, rendered incapable of taking in the sheer immensity of Nature's manifold, are overwhelmed, resulting in an estimation of power which de-centers the viewer into an awareness of his own limited position in the universe—what Paul Crowther has aptly called "existential vertigo."[22] The view, in our immediate perceptual assessment of it, seems a limitless phenomenal mass, utterly unfathomable, and as such the imagination is launched into vain effort to comprehend its magnitude in such a way that leads to the question of the indeterminate (unrepresentable) idea of the infinite.

In short, Kant construes the sublime as occasioned by powers that transcend the phenomenal self and prompt a mode of awe or reverence. The sublime is that which, through the suggestion of perceptually, imaginatively, or emotionally overwhelming properties, succeeds in rendering the scope (and limit) of some human capacity vivid to the senses and opens up a space for encounter with the *noumenon*. He points here to a break between the two dimensions of reality—the phenomenal and the noumenal.

Moreover, for Kant the material limit to our perceptual and rational capacity serves as a kind of *analogue* of total under-

22. Paul Crowther, *The Kantian Sublime: From Morality to Art* (Oxford: Clarendon, 1989).

standing; that is to say, we can never *know* the infinite, but we can imagine it, represent it, think it as an idea, and thus experience the consolation that something transcends the limitations of our phenomenal being (thus for Kant preserving a sense of reason's ability to transcend some vast physicality or infinite power over something so challenging). Yet, that initial experience of the disproportion between the mind's power of ordering and an ungraspable complexity may serve us as an analogue for another situation, one in which we attempt to comprehend something beyond the scope of our understanding—when we find ourselves attempting, for instance, to grasp (to describe and to know) such ideas as God and the Infinite. For Kant, we can never grasp the whole "beyond" this world, limited as we are in the human situation of being in the world; we don't have access to its ultimate Absoluteness. But, as with the sublime, our self-conscious awareness of perceptual and rational limitations is what allows for the reassuring intimation that something transcends finite being.

Of course, the sublime as aesthetic category has its own considerable tradition, itself not lost on Viola. Consider for example, seventeenth-century essayist and poet Joseph Addison, who described this freedom from perceptual confinement in our experiences of the sublime as that which resists the mind's call to order: "Our imagination loves to . . . grasp at anything that is too big for its capacity. We are flung into a pleasing astonishment at such unbounded views, and feel a delightful . . . amazement in the soul at the apprehension of them. The mind of man naturally hates everything that looks like a restraint upon it, and is apt to fancy itself under a sort of confinement."[23] Or here, Edmund Burke in his 1756 treatise, *A Philosophical Inquiry into the Origin of Our Ideas of the Sublime and the Beautiful*, marks the quality of fear and attraction in the sublime, in a psychological calculus of pleasure and pain which relies on a strongly empirical sense of bodily orientation: "Whatever is fitted in any sort to excite the

23. Joseph Addison, *Collected Works, III*, ed. H. Bohn (London, 1890) 397–98.

ideas of pain, and danger, that is to say, whatever is in any sort terrible, or is conversant about terrible objects, or operates in a manner analogous to terror, is a source of the Sublime; that is, it is productive of the strongest emotion which the mind is capable of feeling."[24] In this vain attempt to comprehend infinity, imagination's inadequacy is first experienced as frustration (disturbance, disequilibrium, pain), but then gives way to *pleasure* arising from our awareness that this inadequacy exemplifies the limits of our perceptual ability. Echoing Burke, Kant writes in the *Critique of Judgement*: "The feeling of the sublime is . . . at once a feeling of displeasure, arising from the inadequacy of imagination in the aesthetic estimation of magnitude to attain to its estimation by reason, and a simultaneously awakened pleasure, arising from this very judgement of the inadequacy of the . . . faculty of sense being in accord with reason . . ."[25] Kant's division between the phenomenal and noumenal, or the sensible and the intelligible, further extends to the human self. On the one hand, we are embodied creatures of feeling and sensibility, who think and act in time and space. This means that as phenomenal beings we are part of nature and are subject to determination by nature's causal laws. On the other hand, in so far as it is the human subject which imposes this framework through the categories of the understanding—the forms of intuition (spatio-temporality, causality)—the ultimate self must in some sense be presumed to lie beyond the phenomenal world. It must, in other words, be a noumenal or supersensible self. Thus, as Paul Crowther argues, Kant "gives the supersensible self a negative characterization— namely as that aspect of the self which is not in space and time, and not subject to the categories."[26]

24. Edmund Burke, *A Philosophical Inquiry into the Origin of Our Ideas of the Sublime and the Beautiful* (London: Routledge Classics, 1958, 2008).

25. Kant, *The Critique of Judgement*, trans. and comm. by James Creed Meredith (Oxford, 1952) §27.

26. Crowther, *The Kantian Sublime*, 17.

LYOTARD AND THE POSTMODERN SUBLIME

Jean-François Lyotard's reconstruction and application of the sublime to a theory of contemporary art and new technology is pertinent here. For Lyotard, the sublime (in art) is essential in our postmodern age, in which all legitimizing and stabilizing narratives have been shattered, as it keeps relevant metaphysical thinking (presenting the unpresentable).[27] "That which is not demonstrable is that which stems from Ideas . . . The universe is not demonstrable; neither is humanity, the end of history, the moment, the species, the good, the just, etc.—or, according to Kant, absolutes in general."[28] For Lyotard contemporary art can give new form to Kant's "negative presentation" of the unpresentable; it can make "ungraspable allusions to the invisible within the visible."[29] "The aesthetic of the sublime," Lyotard argues, "is where modern art . . . finds its impetus . . . showing that there is something we can conceive of which we can neither see nor show."[30] The "presence" Lyotard identifies as "a kind of transcendental pre-logic in which thought and sensation are complicit" is prior to an orientation by the categories of the understanding which enable feeling to be thought. This "presence" does not correspond to the ontological order of things in themselves, the immediate apprehension of which was for Lyotard, as for Kant, impossible. The presentation of the sublime, then, is for Lyotard negative; it is, he argues, "compatible with the formless," exceeds the Kantian faculties of imagination, understanding and reason, and is thus freighted with negativity in words like "infinity," "abyss," "unboundedness," "incommensurate, "unconditioned"—it is an awakening of the idea of the supersensible in the subjectivity of contemplation on the sublime. For Lyotard it acknowledges the "desire for the unknown" in the postmodern: "The postmodern would be that

27. Jean-Francois Lyotard, "Presenting the Unpresentable: The Sublime," *Artforum* 20 (April 1992) 64–69.

28. Ibid., 68.

29. Ibid.

30. Ibid.

which, in the modern, puts forward the unpresentable in presentation itself; that which denies the solace of good forms ... that which searches for new presentations, not in order to enjoy them, but in order to impart a stronger sense of the unpresentable."[31]

This sense of the "unseen" is central to Bill Viola's work. It is, I want to call it, a poetics of hope in the as-yet-unsatisfied desire for union and fellowship with the (divine) Other, such that God approaches by withdrawing, or is present by being hidden. It is a God whose presence is felt indirectly; its givenness or grace rests upon our disinterestedness; it is not a product of our will, but prior to it. It involves a *phenomenology* of hope, such that we remain receptively open to the overwhelming *possibility* of the "appearance" of God (a God prior to Being, a pre-ontological God).

VIOLA AND THE UNSEEN PASSIONS

I want to return here to Viola's work jumping ahead some twenty years in the artist's chronology and to a much more recent series of installations collectively titled *The Passions*, which the artist began in 2000 and which takes the form of more than twenty video pieces variously connected by the theme of extreme emotion, and collectively aimed at conveying fundamental but inarticulate human states of being: love, hope, sorrow, death, and regeneration. Much of this series, and other even more recent work, is indebted to Viola's studies in the 1990s of Western art, particularly Medieval and Renaissance devotional painting. Far more than modern re-stagings of art history, these deceptively spare video and sound installations go beyond representation to pursue the ancient theme of revelation of the layers of human consciousness, challenging a viewer's preconditioned expectations and viewing patterns. Most were shot on 35mm film at very high speed and slowed down drastically, so that almost

31. From *The Postmodern Condition*, quoted in Graham Ward, *Theology and Contemporary Critical Theory* (New York: St. Martin's Press, 1996, 2000) 137–38.

imperceptible shifts can be observed; these are then transferred to digital video and played on flat screens. Viola himself explains that these works are meant "for cultivating knowledge of how to be in the world, for going through life. It is useful for developing a deeper understanding, in a very personal, subjective, private way, of your own experiences."[32]

In a sub-group of *The Passions*, the "Quintet" series—*The Quintet of the Astonished, The Quintet of Remembrance, The Quintet of the Silent* and *The Quintet of the Unseen*—Viola presents four groups of five figures in individual videos to explore the universal human emotions of sorrow, pain, anger, fear and joy.[33] In a slow-motion replay that seems to inhabit a space-time all its own, and resulting in exaggerated gesture and expression, Viola captures, as he puts it, "what the old masters didn't paint"—that is, the in-between of emotion that springs from beneath the visible surface of observable phenomena.

In each of the four works that comprise the *Quintet* series, five people are positioned close together as they collectively and individually experience a wave of intense emotion that threatens to overtake each of them. As the sequence begins, their neutral expressions begin to change, at first nearly imperceptibly—but made visible through extreme slow motion—as the emotion, different for each person, overwhelms the group and surges to an acute level. After peaking it subsides, leaving each person thoroughly depleted, physically and psychologically. While in close proximity throughout the experience, the five individuals undergo the rising emotional energy independently with little no acknowledgment or direct interaction with each other. Moreover, the group stands before an empty background with no narrative context or reference to the outside world.

32. *Bill Viola: The Passions*, exhibition catalogue, ed. John Walsh (Los Angeles: Getty, 2003) 75.

33. It is inspired by the four figures surrounding the fifth figure of Christ in Hieronymus Bosch's painting of c. 1490–1500, *Christ Mocked* (*The Crowning of Thorns*).

Five Angels

Another five-part work, again a sub-group within the *Passions* project, is *Five Angels for the Millennium*, 2001, and consists of five individual video sequences showing a clothed man plunging into a pool of water: *Departing Angel, Birth Angel, Fire Angel, Ascending Angel,* and *Creation Angel.* Playing simultaneously and continuously repeating, the images are projected directly onto the walls of a large dark room. As John Walsh describes in the Getty exhibition catalogue:

> The "angel" in each appears infrequently on each screen, breaking through the surface in a sudden explosion of light and sound that interrupts an otherwise peaceful watery landscape. Weightless and motionless, the human figure enters into the depths of a mysterious underwater world, a luminous void of unknown dimensions, where the laws of physics seem suspended and the borders between the infinite cosmos and the finite human body merge.[34]

Long attracted to the transformative and reflective—and symbolic—properties of water, the artist explores the ways in which water sustains, blesses, and takes life away. The video sequences in this work are slow and meditative, and take considerable time and patience to absorb, wherein the viewer is overwhelmed by sensory experience in the darkened room. In our following the illusion of the images—or attempting to—Viola explores how the limits of the image and its manipulations of space and time force us to reevaluate what we have seen; we are left positioned on the boundary between the visible and the invisible, or more accurately, we are left within the invisibility of the once seen (the angel) and the anticipation and knowledge of its return.[35] Amidst a swelling and ebbing soundtrack and unsynchronized percussions of figures striking the water's surface and plunging beneath

34. Ibid., 146.

35. See Donald Kuspit, "Bill Viola: Deconstructing Presence," Barbara London, ed. Bill Viola (New York: Museum of Modern Art, 1987) 73–80.

it, Viola creates, as the artist himself describes it, "an enveloping emotional experience like that of a church."[36]

JEAN-LUC MARION AND THE SATURATED PHENOMENON AS THEOLOGICAL SUBLIME

In reckoning with the idea of representing the invisible, Bill Viola's art can be situated within postmodern notions of the "unrepresentable." Theologically this invokes the idea of seeing God in "glimpses" or "traces," never knowing God completely. Moreover, the apophatic description of God as an abstract experience, not conceptually definable in terms of space and location, nor confinable to conventions of time—God as transcendent of essence—and can be theorized within the context of "unknowability" and Jean-Luc Marion's "God without Being." Central to Marion's thinking—and its pertinence to this study—is the distinction between what he characterizes as the *idol* and the *icon*.

Marion's theory of the *icon* is a theory of the way the invisible (unseen) reveals itself, and as such the icon is defined in opposition to the *idol*. A thing or being becomes an idol when the human gaze directed toward it allows itself to be completed or satisfied by this visible thing or being. The "idol" is essentially an image or confirming concept of God. The intention of the human gaze is completely absorbed in the sight/site of the idol. This means that intention and gaze allow themselves to be fixed on a given visible shape. As Victor Kal as argued, intention and gaze do not *see through* the visible; rather, they are enraptured *with* the visible.[37] Thus the idol is the image of God adjusted to human, finite standards. "The idol," Marion himself states in *God Without*

36. Ibid., 48. In fact, this extended piece, *Five Angels*, is perhaps most reminiscent of Viola's earlier 1996 single projection installation, *The Messenger*, commissioned by and installed at Durham Cathedral. That controversial piece begins similarly in portentous darkness; then, initial lights appear. These begin to coalesce into a form that eventually takes the shape of a man rising up from the depths of water until finally he breaks the surface with a gasp, only to fall back into the dark depths until the cycle begins again.

37. Bulhof and ten Kate, eds., *Flight of the Gods*, 157.

Being, "consigns the divine to the measure of a human gaze."[38] As a result, the gaze creates the idol, and the onlooker is fully satisfied by what he sees. This way of seeing Marion calls idolatry. The idol is created by desire to see and fixes what is seen; the idol is exactly there where the gaze stops, and as such, the idol is like a mirror; it is merely reflecting my desires—does not allow a "beyond." That which is reflected is the gaze itself, the gaze obsessed *by* itself. I see nothing but my own gaze. The idol may be the image of God, but cut to the size of the human imagination. Philosophically, the idol takes the shape of an idea or concept—and conceptualization means assimilation by human imagination.[39]

The *icon*, by contrast, represents a non-conceptual, non-idolized "appearance" of God. The icon, again as Victor Kal puts it, is not produced by the human gaze; rather, "the icon summons a gaze."[40] The theology of the icon, Marion claims, is found in Colossians 1:15: "He is the image of the invisible God . . ." The *icon* overcomes the mirror and the intentional gaze, and itself claims the gaze of the onlooker. In other words, the visible icon, *qua* object, refers *beyond itself* to the invisible: "The icon does not make the invisible *tangibly* present. The icon makes the invisible *as invisible* present for the glance. The icon can be seen and refers beyond itself." [41] As Marion argues in *The Crossing of the Visible*: "In the idol, the gaze of man is frozen in its mirror; in the icon, the gaze of man is lost in the invisible gaze that visibly engages him." The icon "unbalances human sight in order to engulf it in infinite depth," it is about the "presence of a non-object."[42] I do not focus upon it, rather it focuses on me. The icon is the intentional

38. Jean-Luc Marion, *God Without Being*, trans., T. Carlson (Chicago: University of Chicago Press, 1991).

39. Peter Jonkers and Rudd Welten, eds., *God in France: Eight Contemporary French Thinkers on God* (Leuven: Peeters, 2005) 190–91.

40. Ibid.,158.

41. Ibid.

42. Jean-Luc Marion, *The Crossing of the Visible*, trans. James K. A. Smith (Stanford: Stanford University Press, 2004) 60–61.

gaze of the other in me; he refers to it as the "perfect reversal" of intentionality. The icon approaches me, it *gives* itself.[43]

This is precisely what I think is occurring in Viola's *Quintets* and, more specifically perhaps, his *Observance*. In *Observance*, from 2002, a steady stream of people slowly moves forward toward us, solemnly and ritualistically. One by one, they pause at the head of the line, overcome with emotion. Their gazes are trained on an unknown object or unseen tragedy just out of sight below the edge of the frame, some soliciting force operating within "our" space. Sometimes gently touching or occasionally exchanging brief glances between them as they pass, all are unified by their common desire to reach the front of the line and make contact with what/whomever is there, effecting a "crossing of gazes" as Marion would have it, two currents of consciousness pressing upon each other—recognizing separation and alienation while desiring to overcome it. What occurs here is the viewer's receptiveness to the world that, coming from the "other," resounds in him. We are open to being "caught upon" by the image, instead of having authority of visual possession over it; we are called into an aesthetic posture of attentiveness. Like Marion's icon, these images preserve transcendence by refusing the mirroring function of the idol, such that the viewer finds himself envisaged by the other.

Central also to Marion's phenomenology is the idea of the "saturated phenomenon," and it is that which can be tied directly to our extended sense of the Kantian sublime. Marion's "saturated phenomenon" is, as John Caputo has described it, "the idea that there are phenomena of such overwhelming givenness or overflowing fulfillment that the intentional acts [such as conscious efforts at conceptualization . . .] aimed at these phenomena are overrun, flooded—or saturated."[44] Marion, thus, can be situated within the earlier discussion about the (im)possibility of "nam-

43. Jonkers and Welten, eds., *God in France*, 192–93.

44. John Caputo, "Marion, Jean-Luc, *The Erotic Phenomenon*," trans. Stephen E. Lewis, book review in *Ethics* 118 (1) 164.

ing" God—a recovery, that is, of apophatic theological language, the "excess of significance."

But how, one must ask, after post-modernism does one speak of God? A god who is not the result of theoretical constructions or psychological desires?

Marion's *God Without Being*, as Christina Gschwandtner's recent account argues, was just such an attempt to think God without or beyond the language of being or ontology. "Traditional metaphysical language," she posits, "that has been used to speak of God is inadequate to such a task."[45] It is this critique of metaphysics, and indeed of presence, which links Marion to his former teacher Derrida, and to the postmodern critique of *logos* and failure of metaphysics generally. For Marion, such efforts to designate God philosophically as ultimate being not only fail by their inadequacy in speaking of a divine, but can even be considered idolatrous.[46] In other words, God cannot be an object of human knowledge, an essence the human subject can comprehend with any degree of certainty—such a knowing would, Marion argues, subordinate God as object to the epistemological demands of a knower. Such a knowing ego which grounds all reality within a "metaphysics of presence" involves the notion that the world can be divided into such subject-object relations; it posits a world made up of objects the attributes of which, and therefore names and descriptions, can be predicated. Hence, Marion's language of incomprehensibility, blinding light, *saturation* and *excess*, which diverges from Derrida and his deconstructionist acolytes as fullness does from emptiness.

Marion develops a phenomenality that is "saturated" or fulfilled—abundant phenomenon. This means it does not depend on my orientation or my intentionality or my interpretation. It blinds me, overriding my intentionality. Marion characterized it as a *surplus*, or *excess*: again, it blinds me; there is too much light.

45. Christina Gschwandtner, *Reading Jean-Luc Marion: Exceeding Metaphysics* (Bloomington: Indiana University Press, 2007) 3.

46. Ibid.

"The spiritual light," wrote St. John of the Cross, "is so bright and so transcendent that it blinds . . ."[47] Darkness here is the excess of light, rather than its absence. The "sublime," as formulated by Kant, similarly represents a saturated phenomenon.

Metaphysics for Marion is idolatrous precisely because it circumscribes the divine by a concept, a concept that supposes it can define—and thereby limit—God. And the notion of excess or saturation is not unlike the initial disappointment the mind experiences in the Kantian sublime wherein one is confronted with the limits of finite consciousness. In an interview with Richard Kearney, author of *The God Who May Be* (2001), Marion speaks of this sense of disappointment: "The very experience of the excess of intuition over signification makes clear that the excess may be felt and expressed as disappointment. The experience of disappointment means that I marked an experience which I cannot understand, because I have no concept of it. So the excess and the disappointment can come together."[48] This "disappointment" is the situation of encountering something without having the possibility to understand it. It is an invitation not to comprehension, but to *participation.*

But is God/the Divine Other, then, too transcendent, without possibility for relationship? This is the question or critique Richard Kearney puts to Marion, arguing instead for a *revelation* of God that doesn't speculate about Being or ontology but rather remarks on the experience of plenitude, and therefore the idea of a god of possibility and promise, a more hopeful notion than that which he ascribes to Marion as "a divinity so far beyond-being that no heurmeneutics of interpreting, imagining, symbolizing, or narrativizing is really acceptable," where "God's alterity appears so utterly unnameable and apophatic that any attempt to throw heurmeneutic drawbridges between it and our finite means of language is deemed a form of idolatry."[49] Such negative,

47. Kavanaugh, *Collected Works*, 434.

48. Quoted in Gschwandtner, *Reading Jean-Luc Marion*, 78.

49. Ibid., 98.

apophatic theology, Kearney claims, denies any possibility of narrative imagination, such that "the divine remains utterly unthinkable, unnamable, unrepresentable—that is, unmediatable."

While this notion of the abjectness (and preclusion) of God may well be present in Derrida and postmodernist reveling in the bankruptcy of language as representation, Marion, I think, may be closer to our mystics in arguing not merely about this inadequacy but, despite it, urging us to imagine nevertheless—to trust in a revelation and to be open to overwhelming promise of grace. Yet Kearney's critique is helpful for our purposes in articulating what is going on in Bill Viola's construction of just such an aesthetic—and theological—posture of *attentiveness*. Kearney insists, as Gschwantdner points out, on a need for what he calls a "narrative heurmeneutics," according to which "religious language"—and I count Viola's efforts as such—"endeavor to say something (however hesitant and provisional) about the unsayable."[50] Viola's work, as such, opens our eyes to a new way for things one would not otherwise see—a theology (and technology) of *revelation*. Yet, I would still maintain that Marion's phenomenology of possibility is just such an aesthetics of *hope*. As Marion scholar Rudd Welten nicely concludes: "Marion will not show us God; he just makes sure there is room for God to show Himself! Thus, Marion emphasizes the difference between appearance and perception. Something appearing does not a priori urge me to perceive it!"[51]

50. Ibid.

51. Jonkers and Welten, eds., *God in France*, 206.

5

The Pursuit of Beauty vs. the Aesthetics of Worldmakers

Arthur Pontynen

THE TITLE OF THIS collection of essays, based on a recent CAA conference session of the same name, is: "Beyond Belief: Theo-esthetics or Old-time Religion." To my reading, that session title brings to our attention three primary points to consider. First it posits that the Modernist tradition centers on an alienation of religion from art, an alienation that results in a fragmented and oppositional culture of cynicism and irony. Second, it asks if a new theo-aesthetic humanism may be emerging as a remedy to that malaise. And third, it speculates whether that new theo-aesthetic humanism—one that is belief-less—can provide space for a healing numinous presence in contemporary postmodern culture.

The conclusion of this paper is that it cannot. Indeed, rather than being the remedy to what ails us, it is in fact the very source of our malady. It will presently be argued that the notion of a belief-less theo-aesthetic humanism results not in a renewed culture of integration and unification, but rather a culture informed by cynicism, irony, and ultimately, violence. It is a failed Postmodernist response to a failed Modernist paradigm.

This paper hopes to establish that the notion of a belief-less theo-aesthetic humanism is historically grounded in the assumptions of the Baroque. Specifically, it is the Baroque redefinition of science and reason that leads to the so-called Enlightenment and its off-spring the Modernist-Postmodernist tradition. That redefinition leads to a theo-aesthetic humanism beyond belief—but that conclusion is neither healing nor numinous. Rather, it is a conclusion we have seen before; it is but a return to that failed theology now called Existentialism and once called paganism.

In its stead this essay will offer a different and optimistic alternative, one that affirms the numinous without succumbing to the perennial folly of Existentialist and pagan violence.

As noted above it is the Baroque redefinition of science that leads to the so-called Enlightenment and its offspring, the Modernist-Post-modernist tradition. That redefining of science—and thus also of reason—was prompted by the crisis faced by the scientific rationalism of Scholasticism. That crisis was intrinsic and extrinsic: the Conceptualist splitting of ontological and human reason, and the positivist limitation of knowledge to fact. The Baroque redefining of science by Francis Bacon and reason by Rene Descartes resulted in the development of a new scientific rationalism that is foundational to Modernists following Kant, and Postmodernists responding to Kant, such as Kierkegaard, Hegel, Marx, and Nietzsche.

To the point: Modernists and Postmodernists share a ground in the Baroque redefinition of science and reason; that redefinition has resulted in the false dichotomy of a science-based culture vs. a religion-based culture. It is a dichotomy that is not grounded in reality, but in a particular, recent, and flawed philosophy. That philosophy is referred to as the Enlightenment, which afflicts us to the present—with terrible results.[1]

According to Scholasticism, science is referred to by the term *scientia*, an intellectual discipline that offers knowledge of more than facts. That is, both physics and metaphysics are considered objects of knowledge. Religion and ethics are viewed by

1. See Arthur Pontynen, "Beauty and the Enlightened Beast," *American Outlook* (July/August, 2001) 37ff.

scientia as things to be understood. Religion and ethics center on the pursuit of knowledge of what is true and good in reality. They center on the pursuit of wisdom—of *sapientia*—and of beauty.

But during the Baroque *scientia* was redefined as *scientism*, or more precisely, knowledge was newly limited to descriptive facts. Consequently neither religion nor ethics could remain as objects of knowledge. That is, the objective pursuit of knowledge of what is true and good in reality was newly limited to the pursuit of facts, of accurate descriptions. Science, religion and culture once centered on the obtaining of wisdom—the splendor of which is beauty; now they are reduced to a matter of aesthetics, of fact and emotional response.

That shift to facts and emotional response affects our understanding of reason as well. In place of reason being capital 'L' Logos, that is, the *reason* for the world and life rightly being as they ought to be, reason is newly limited to small 'l' logos—as mere logical clarity or consistency. Reason shifts from the pursuit of wisdom to the pursuit of analytical coherence, rational formalism, and strategies of power. We can pursue a freedom and virtue denying equality, a coarse materialistic pragmatism, or a violent authenticity.

Therein lies the problem: for reality and life to be meaningful, we must go beyond mere facts, rationalized feelings, and power. We must rise from the realm of descriptive *what* to that of an explanatory *why*. We must seek to understand a numinous reality. But such numinous narratives are beyond the ken of *scientism*.

This Modernist reduction of science to fact, and reason to logical clarity, grounded in equality, is referred to as Positivism. Via the pursuit of a Positivist scientific-rationalism we reach the age of Enlightenment in which it is assumed that fact and logic will permit us to escape from superstition, ignorance, and religion. Following Bacon and Newton we should seek facts, following Descartes we should seek logical clarity, and following Kant we should attempt to combine the two by constructing fact-based rational narratives. We either live in a world of mere facts, or we construct narratives according to the structure of our minds.

This results in a radical shift in Western culture. Instead of seeking objective truth in the attempt to rise above the confusion of disconnected facts and the banality of mere descriptions, we should now either be satisfied with mere facts (materialism) or we should *construct* paradigms of understanding (Modernism). In other words, we should be Nominalists or Constructivists.

But this allegedly secular shift results not in the denial of metaphysics, but rather, in the advocacy of a new and violent metaphysics. Nominalism and Constructivism tacitly promote several metaphysical assertions: 1) that the world is comprised only of meaningless facts, 2) that we can use those facts to construct—and deconstruct—our worlds, and therefore 3) that the world and our lives have no objective purpose or meaning— beyond our will to power.

The alleged secularization of science and reason by Nominalism and Constructivism results then in a self-deification where knowledge of reality conforms to our minds and wills. We are, to use Nelson Goodman's term, *worldmakers*.[2] Therein lies either irony or brute cynicism: instead of seeking Truth or God, we are now called upon to be Gods.

The Positivist Auguste Comte asserts that we should abandon traditional attempts to rise from facts to meaning, from *what* to *why*. Rather, we should recognize that the realm of *why* is myth, to be escaped by clinging to the realm of *what*. However, in that world of facts, he advises, we should remake the world—and others.

The Modernist Kant recognizes that the Positivist denial of the realm of *why* destroys both understanding and morality. He attempts to reconnect fact with meaning via human reason. But in declaring that the facts of reality conform to our minds—that we construct our knowledge of reality—he relegates knowledge

2. Nelson Goodman, *Ways of Worldmaking* (Indianapolis: Hackett, 1988).

and morality to being the product of our minds. Once again, the conclusion is not secularization, but self-deification.

By limiting knowledge to facts, Modernists and Postmodernists claim to know what they cannot know: that there is no objective meaning in the universe and life. There is no Truth, Goodness, or Beauty to find. This is a crucial point: the assertion that the Enlightenment and Modernism escape taking a metaphysical stance is patently false. Modernist-Postmodernist art and culture are merely religious in a different way. *Their religion is Existentialism, in which we are all purposeless truth incarnate.* We are theo-aesthetic humanists.

So Nominalists and Constructivists claim to know what their science cannot know: that reality and life have no purpose, that there is no *why*. Therefore, Positivist scientism necessarily has a religious component and that religion is *beyond belief*. That is, instead of belief being grounded in wisdom, it is now grounded in the will. Following Rousseau, comfort is sought in assuming that will to be good, but how can a good will be recognized if goodness is subjective? A will lacking a grounding in ontological wisdom is by definition arbitrary, unintelligible, and violent. Kant's assumption that we can recognize good will even though goodness is unknowable makes no sense. Nietzsche concludes: we then operate beyond good and evil—but then goodness is denied.

That is the core of a willful, a belief-less, a theo-aesthetic humanism. We ought to play god by manipulating material facts to suit our desires, be they trivial or a matter of identity. The Postmodernist secularist is indistinguishable from the Postmodernist religionist: Truth or God is the product of our imagination. In either case the result is a religion grounded in an intellectually purposeless humanism that centers on the will. The required religion of Positivism—and therefore of the Modernist-Postmodernist tradition—is Existentialism—be it grounded in individualism, or in race, gender, or economic class. Truth or God is not objective, is not Being, to which we freely aspire. Rather, it is subjective, it is becoming, of which we partake.

Now if Existentialism is true (which is an ironic notion in itself), then virtually all of the fine art produced before the Modernist era around the world must be false. Therefore all art around the world and through the ages produced in the pursuit of wisdom and beauty—are lies. This astounding arrogance goes virtually unnoticed as we memorize facts and (de)construct meaning. But then the fine arts are thus relegated to entertainment, therapy, or propaganda.

To the point: as *worldmakers*, religion is not denied; it is immanentized. We are both the creators and destroyers of our worlds and the worlds of others. Being, or Truth is us becoming. Indeed, the primary advocates of the Modernist-Postmodernist tradition—Kant, Hegel, Feuerbach, Fichte, Marx, Comte, Nietzsche, Sartre, Heidegger, and more—all advocate that humanity play the role of god. Whether such advocacy is to be taken ironically, cynically, or authentically matters not. The political and cultural consequences remain. Practically speaking, behind the mask of Modernist scientific rationality is a willful self-deification. And on this point both the Postmodernist Theodor Adorno and the Christian Thomas Molnar agree: the wish to construct and deconstruct the self—and others—is intrinsically violent and sadistic.

It is without any exaggeration that the Modernist reductionistic redefinition of science as *scientism* necessitates that each of us play God—and hence we can choose to conform or destroy. Sanitized under the rubrics *creativity, constructivism, self-realization, authenticity* and *inner necessity*, we each and all are to be—as Nelson Goodman calls them—*worldmakers*. In a world of facts we construct—and deconstruct—reality and humanity. We are deemed creative in a world without objective purpose or truth. But creativity without truth is less than idiotic—it is sheer brutality. Therefore art and scholarship can only be nihilistic or totalitarian. We are demigods and demagogues whose wills violently compete or conform on a purposeless playing field.

This world-making and world-destroying is grounded in inner necessity, a concept that resonates in both German Idealism and French Romanticism. The scholarly sources advocating just such a self-deification are multiple. They are grounded in the repeated claim that inner necessity[3] trumps both science and reason. It is inner necessity that warrants our constructing realities—but it can also be inner necessity that warrants our deconstructing the realities of others. Both Constructivism and Deconstructivism result in a worshiping of purposeless willfulness. It requires that we worship Pride.

It is cause for alarm then that Constructivism/Deconstructivism is taken for granted by the academic mainstream today. It is foundational to a variety of academic taboos: one cannot question tolerance, cultural relativism, multiculturalism, or authenticity—at least the authenticity of the oppressed. To depart from Constructivism/Deconstructivism is to risk professional survival. It is to commit heresy against the Modernist-Postmodernist articles of faith.

Consequently, elite Western culture is now grounded in violence, be it the nihilism and totalitarianism of the Left—or the Right. That violence is found in the conflicts between Constructivism and Deconstructivism, between Individualism and Communitarianism, and between the advocates of Tolerance and Authenticity. We cannot champion both tolerance and authenticity—without engaging in violence. And it matters not whether we consider ourselves to be secular or religious, conservative or liberal. The Modernist-Postmodernist tradition is the means by which we now experience existence—and willfully affect the existence of others.

That violent process of Constructivism/Deconstructivism is rationalized as a dialectic of progress in which the ultimate goal is the liberation of the oppressed. What is offered the oppressed? The realization of inner necessity, be it individually based or

---

3. Inner necessity permeates postmodernist thought. For example, see: Wilhelm Worringer, *Abstraction and Empathy* (Cleveland: Meridian, 1967). See also Arthur Pontynen, "Facts, Feelings, and (In)coherence vs. The Pursuit of Beauty (Kandinsky and Florensky)," *St. Vladimir's Theological Quarterly* 40/3 (1996).

grounded in race, gender, economic class, or creed. But of course, self-realization in a meaningless world cannot be achieved. In a meaningless world self-realization collapses in a nihilistic void.

So there are deadly contradictions within a belief-less theo-aesthetic humanism, a purposeless freedom, a tolerant authenticity, a willful culture. Such self-contradictory qualities have resulted in the unparalleled carnage of religious warfare. Let's be clear on this point: the most terrible religious warfare starts in the Baroque period, continues through the Enlightenment, and blossoms with unparalleled carnage in the allegedly secular Modernist twentieth century. Nearly 100 million people killed. It is during the reign of a Positivist scientific-rationalism that the most dreadful violence occurred. *World-making* has a terrible price, the price of pride.

Nonetheless, Modernism and Postmodernism now brutally dominate the academy. Allegedly tolerant and diverse, that academy uniformly rejects the notion of seeking truth, goodness, and beauty. That tolerance and diversity is violently hostile to the pursuit of truth, goodness, and beauty. A sure way to provoke that violence is to ask a simple question: are the truth claims of works of fine art—particularly obviously religious fine art—true? To ask if fine art to some degree effectively explains reality and life—to ask if fine art is numinous—is to provoke the wrath of the Modernist and the Postmodernist. While posturing as advocates of tolerance and diversity, they enforce with an iron fist a singularly relativist and aesthetic worldview. That worldview is one in which belief is redefined as the product of the will—the will to power. Belief no longer seeks knowledge of objective Truth or Being. Belief is us becoming.

So what then is the good news? Despite the power of a politicized peer review that limits dissent, dissent to this Modernist-Postmodernist paradigm is long and continuing.[4]

4. See my article, "A Winter Landscape: Reflections on the Theory and Practice of Art History," *Art Bulletin* (September, 1986). More recently, see Robert Williams, "A Newer Protagoras," *Art Bulletin* (September, 2006). In his introduction he offers a stunning comment: "Protagoras, who, as a Sophist, can

Indeed, a previous New Humanism was advocated particularly by American scholars who keenly perceived the fatal flaws of Modernism and Postmodernism.

At the turn of the twentieth century those scholars and artists formed a New Humanist movement specifically dedicated to escaping the tragedy of Modernism. Major figures within that movement were Irving Babbitt, Royal Cortissoz, A Phillip McMahon, Kenyon Cox, Frank Jewett Mather, Ivor Winters; their concerns were later advanced by Alan Bloom, Alasdair McIntyre, Thomas Molnar, and others.[5]

What these scholars offer is a stunningly precise and articulate critique of the cultural malaise resulting from the Modern-Postmodern tradition. These figures were or are brilliant analysts of culture who despite their trenchant debunking of Modernism were unable to provide a foundation for restoring a culture dedicated to the free and responsible pursuit of truth, goodness, and beauty. Space does not permit a presenting of their detailed critiques. They share a rejection of the notions of German Idealism and French Romanticism. Those cultural paradigms are rejected because they are anti-intellectual, anti-cultural, and violent. But what these scholars do not provide is a remedy to their dominance. They make clear the dysfunctionalism of Modernism and Postmodernism but fail to provide a viable alternative.

Academic politics have played a role in that failure. An intrinsically willful existentialist academy is hostile to rational dialogue and those who promote it. But another reason for this failure is their neglect in contesting the limitation of knowledge to facts. Not offering an alternative understanding of science, they floundered in the impossibility of reconciling the pursuit of Truth and Wisdom with the Nominalist and Positivist pursuit

---

be taken to represent the fact that so much of the modern thought on which contemporary art history depends betrays a deep affinity with Sophistry."

5. In the field of art history see also, Arthur Pontynen, *For the Love of Beauty: Art, History, and the Moral Foundations of Aesthetic Judgment* (New Brunswick, NJ: Transaction, 2006).

of facts and power. They failed to reconcile *why* with a paradigm that could only understand *what*.

Consequently, scholarship and art is controlled by those who do not believe in science and reason in the pursuit of ontological Truth. By assuming that meaning is grounded not in reason and wisdom, but in the will of worldmakers, they are impervious to rational argument. They are then trapped in an anti-intellectual solipsism—and so are we.

What then is the positive solution? Let us conclude by returning to the core phrase of this collection of essays: *Beyond belief: a theo-aesthetic new humanism.* That is the crux of the matter: what is the nature and relationship of belief, theology, aesthetics, and humanism?

To the Greek mind—at least that of Plato and Aristotle—belief ought to be grounded in knowledge and knowledge ought to be grounded in purposeful and thus intelligible reality. We ought to believe what is true in reality. But since the Baroque, belief is beyond the realm of such knowledge. It is found in facts and feelings; we are empiricists and mystics. We don't need to know about reality, we just need to experience our realities. The empiricist and the mystic go hand in hand in that both reject the importance of ontological reason. So the new mysticism is grounded in our own will. Existentialism is a narcissistic type of mysticism.

Correspondingly, *theo-aesthetics* refers to how *why* and *what* are to be combined. The Greek *theo* literally refers to an objective idealism, to objective Truth or God; to seek Truth is to seek knowledge of *why* things happen as they ought. In contrast, the Greek term *aesthesis* literally refers to materialism, to facts, to the realm of *what*. *Theo-esthetics* refers then to how meaning and facts, how *why* and *what*, are rightly combined. It refers to truth being made manifest in the material world.

Within the Classical tradition the relationship of *what* and *why* refers to the relationship of material fact and Being. There is the world of things (matter or fact), the realm of existing things

(Ta Onta) comprised of matter and fact informed with structure, and the immaterial realm of a transcendent thing (Ta On), which provides the source for that structure and meaning as such. In seeking wisdom we attempt to rise from nominalist fact, to structured fact, and ultimately strive to obtain a glimpse of the source of that structure, the objective *why,* or *reason,* or *Being* itself.

This resonates with the Judeo-Christian tradition in which the why of the universe, is presented in Exodus 3:14: "I Am that I Am" (the Hebrew phrase is: *'ehyeh 'asher 'ehyeh*); and significantly, that Being is directly associated with Reason or Logos in the Christian text John 1 and with a human being—Christ. It is both transcendently objective, and immanent and incarnate. It is a Theo-centric rather than a Theo-aesthetic humanism that is offered.

In conclusion: As I am sure many readers already know, there is a wide variety of humanistic traditions historically and currently available. In the West the Classical-Judeo-Christian humanism of Augustine is foundationally distinct to those of the Scholastic Aquinas, the Positivist Comte, the Communist Marx, and the Existentialist Sartre. There is even the old humanism of Plato, Aristotle, and Erasmus, the new humanism of Irving Babbitt and Paul Elmer More, and the current new new humanism of John Dewey and the signers of the new Humanist Manifesto of 1933.

Correspondingly there is a wide variety of scientific traditions historically and currently available. As Thomas Kuhn makes clear, those who assume the permanence and inevitability of Positivism are naive of the historical changes concerning what constitutes science.[6]

To the point, the Positivist mind can only perceive humanism as grounded in sociological fact and willful preference. It is a humanism that is beyond meaningful belief—since its beliefs are grounded in mere fact and will. It is a belief lacking understand-

---

6. Thomas Kuhn, *The Structure of Scientific Revolutions* (Chicago: University of Chicago Press, 1970).

ing since understanding must be grounded in ontological reality. As such, this new humanism is not so new after all. It is a return to Paganism with its long and miserable pedigree. In contrast, there is the humanism that perennially aspires to be grounded not in fact or will but the ontologically ideal. Within that type of humanism we are not world makers but wisdom seekers. So we are faced with two options: a violent neo-pagan theo-aesthetic humanism in which we are gods, or a different kind of humanism in which we seek God or Truth.

For the Positivist, humanism can only be understood existentially—we merely exist. As such we are incarnate yet purposeless gods. So as understood via Positivism a theo-aesthetic new humanism beyond belief is a paean to a narcissistic mystical humanism which collapses within its own pagan violence.

In contrast, a non-Positivist theo-centric humanism is not really new. It is the Pre-Scholastic heritage of Western Civilization, a civilization that remains today as precious as it is fragile. That practical pursuit of ontological wisdom is a reconciliation of becoming with Being. That is the scientific and rational substance of the Doctrine of the Incarnation.

As a matter of knowledge, not feeling or faith, that doctrine intellectually affirms the realm of Being, including human being. As such it holds particular human values to be grounded in reality, not a willful violence. Those are transcendent in justification, and immanent in realization. Just as the Doctrine of the Incarnation affirms our humanity, it denies our narcissism. It denies our claims of self-deification. It affirms also the practical pursuit of truth, goodness, and beauty—while on this earth. The Doctrine of the Incarnation affirms the pursuit of science, reason, and fine art since all combine *what* and *why* via the use of reason in the pursuit of wisdom. It thus affirms a humanistic culture of responsible freedom.

But this theo-centric humanist doctrine, so essential to the advocacy of human rights and scientific rationality, now suffers the Postmodernist gaze, a gaze that can only see its own dismal metaphysics of death. Nonetheless, for those who believe in the ontological reality of human rights, and the free and responsible pursuit of the True, Good, and Beautiful, then this long neglected doctrine warrants new scientific, rational, and cultural consideration.

6

A Secular Trinity?

The Transformation of Christian Iconography in a Post-Christian Age

MICHELLE LANG

THE CONTEMPORARY VISUAL ARTS have few theoretical links to religion—theological aesthetics is relevant to traditional Christians only and art history has neither the framework, nor the inclination, to address religious and spiritual issues that are not safely located in the past. But art continues to use various strategies to express our relationship to the numinous, including representations of God that can be understood as secularized versions of the Christian Trinity. These images are grounded in theologies that recognize contemporary scientific theory and the realities of postmodern Western culture, replacing the common deistic, dialogic, monarchical and agential theories of the relationship between God and the world with more organic models, where the divine is both transcendent and immanent, and where the Christian Trinity can be formulated in less denotative, patriarchal, terms as the Creator God, the Incarnate God, and the Sanctifying God. This loosening of traditional Christian iconography creates a space for the spiritual content of art to reference this still-dominant religious paradigm without being confined by its dogma.

Before this subject can be addressed, a few words on terminology. Where the term "God" is not used here in the context of the argument of a particular author, it refers to a general, and I admit, relatively undefined, Christian concept of deity. For instance, John Hick's idea of non- or post-traditional Christianity, which is informed by the ethics of Jesus, but is only one of many paths to spiritual enlightenment, positing a generic viewer for whom Christianity is more a cultural backdrop than a specific practice—what I term the "casual Christian."[1] This seems to be a large group, even in this country. Although 82% of American adults in a 2007 Harris Poll claimed to believe in God, only 25% went to church once week or more, and 40% attend once a year or less.[2]

Traditional, dogmatic Christianity produces little scholarship specifically on art; apparently this is due more to indifference than hostility.[3] Many believers feel that fine art is unacceptably elitist, and that the subject of personal taste is embarrassingly trivial for a so-called good Christian, particularly since the Bible has little to say on the subject.[4] While there is more interaction between more liberal Christianity and the visual arts, an essential gulf still exists between a faith-based worldview, and the secular, professional production and study of the arts. For example, many Christian writers are still concerned that the products of human creativity are appreciated too much for their own sake—that an aesthetic experience is confused with a spiritual one. This in turn is seen to result in what Friedheim Mennekes describes as "the

1. John Hick, *The Metaphor of God Incarnate: Christology in a Pluralistic Age*, 2nd ed., (Louisville: Westminster John Knox, 1993) 13.

2. Online: www.harrisinteractive.com, Poll #119, November 29, 2007. Interestingly, only 23% believed the Torah was the word of God.

3. See for example, Hilary Brand and Adrienne Chaplin, *Art and Soul: Signposts for Christians and the Arts* (Carlisle, UK: Solway, 1999) 25.

4. Frank Burch Brown, *Good Taste, Bad Taste, & Christian Taste: Aesthetics in Religious Life* (Oxford: Oxford University Press, 2000) 3, 8.

beginning of a new unattached spirituality which, in its freedom, is badly in need of a methodological-theological thinking through."[5] Gregory Wolfe suggests that at the root of this issue is the "fear of imagination itself—a force that can't be tamed or made to fit into comforting, predictable categories."[6] Although the concept of imagination has been attributed to the Christian God—as in the imaginative power of the Incarnation or the Holy Spirit—it still tends to be seen as irrational and misleading.[7] Consequently, the products of human imagination, and especially those that that rely on visual forms, are threatening. And this viewpoint is only reinforced by the perception of popular, visual culture as decadent and immoral.

At the same time, many Christians who do believe the arts have an important role to play in contemporary religious life lament the aesthetic quality of work produced within the faith. Ena Heller, the Executive Director of the Museum of Biblical Art in New York, admits that much contemporary art with religious content tends to place less emphasis or privilege on artistic talent, and as such, isn't really art.[8] Laurel Gasque suggests that the problem is that the dogma of institutional Christianity requires precise representation—that three centuries of promoting certainty is incompatible with the suggestive and metaphorical nature of artistic expression.[9] The result has been a sterile art that, failing to revive an exhausted iconography, recycles accepted versions of Christian figures and events. The most recognizable image of this type is perhaps Warner Sallman's *Head of Christ* (1940) which,

5. Friedheim Mennekes, "Between Doubt and Rapture—Art and the Church Today: The Spiritual in the Art of the Twentieth Century," *Religion and the Arts* 4 (2000) 182.

6. Gregory Wolfe, *Intruding Upon the Timeless: Meditations on Art, Faith, and Mystery* (Baltimore: Square Halo, 2003) 91.

7. Patrick Sherry, *Spirit and Beauty: An Introduction to Theological Aesthetics* (Oxford: Clarendon, 1992) 122–23.

8. Ena Heller, "Forward," *The Next Generation: Contemporary Expressions of Faith*, exhibition catalogue (New York: Museum of Biblical Art, 2005) 7.

9. Laurel Gasque, "The Christian Stake in the Arts," *CRUX* 35 (1999) 17, 23.

despite many interesting variations, remains the dominant image of Jesus for the average American viewer.

A few Christian churches are concerned with bringing more contemporary visual culture into their worship, but this is not the norm; even liberal congregations tend to find the arts ontologically suspect, if not morally threatening. When St. Paul's Anglican Church in Cardiff offered a *Dr. Who*-themed communion service in September 2007—typically, this was an attempt to attract younger people to the congregation—the story was reported in the national media.[10] In the United States, The Center for Arts, Religion, and Education, founded in 1987, offers courses to students from the Graduate Theological Union—a consortium of nine seminaries, including the Pacific School of Religion in Berkeley, which has a Doctoral Program in Art and Religion, but overall the inclusion of the visual arts in education and worship remains an issue.[11]

The visual arts have also been examined from the perspective of Christian theology. This usually includes a complex discussion of the concept of beauty, and the validity of sense perception and imagination.[12] A few of these scholars focus their attention on those viewers interested in religious and spiritual themes who do not see through the lens of orthodox, traditional, or even practicing Christianity. For Paul Tillich, for example, art is implicitly religious if it is a sincere expression, in any form, of

10. BBC News (bbc.co.uk/go/pr/fr/-/1/hi1/wales/6991351.stm), September 12, 2007.

11. See Ronald Goetz, "Art in Seminary: Revolutionizing Theological Education," *Christian Century* 103 (March 1976) 299–303; James L. Empereur, "How Can the Church Worship in Postmodern Times?" in *Postmodern Worship and the Arts*, Doug Adams and Michael E. Moynahan, ed. (San Jose: Resource Publications, 2002); and Richard Wilkinson, "Missing Persons: Where are All the Great Evangelical Artists?" *Regeneration Quarterly* 2 (Summer 1996) 13–16.

12. On theological aesthetics, see, for example: Richard Viladesau, *Theological Aesthetics* (New York: Oxford University Press, 1999); and Edward Farley, *Faith and Beauty: A Theological Aesthetic* (Aldershot, UK: Ashgate, 2001).

a search for ultimate meaning using traditional symbolism, with this latter aspect being necessary, but not sufficient. Writing in 1960, Tillich acknowledges the use of Christian symbols without asserting that they represent irrefutable truths—his concern is with what he terms "ultimate reality," that which transcends the merely religious.[13] Tillich attempts to bridge a divide that still exists today—between those viewers who understand Christian subjects and symbols as representing an underlying truth in metaphorical form, and those Christians, both liberal and conservative, for whom this material represents the foundation of a worldview. [14]

This divide is illustrated by Doug Adams's 2002 review of William Dyrness's *Visual Faith: Art, Theology and Worship in Dialogue* in *Christian Century* magazine. Adams discusses the Christian meaning in *The Running Fence* (1972–1976) identified by the artists, Christo and Jean-Claude, as a "ribbon of light" that presents the world as a mysterious gift endowed by the Creator.[15] Adams notes that with his temporary, fabric works, Christo references the shroud as a symbol of both death and resurrection, and that by using only his first name, Christo (Javacheff) emphasizes the theological underpinnings of his work, something that his wife Jean-Claude is surprised more critics have failed to notice. In the process, Christo also alludes to the creative power of artists themselves—the presence of the divine incarnated, to a degree, in

13. Paul Tillich, *On Art and Architecture*, John Dillenberger ed. (New York: Crossroad, 1987) 232. In general, Tillich emphasized a radically transcendent, infinite, and unknowable God: the ground of Being.

14. The difficulties inherent in trying to bridge this gap are illustrated in: John W. Dixon Jr., "Art as the Making of the World: Outline of Method in the Criticism of Religion and Art," *Journal of the American Academy of Religion* 5 (1983) 15–36; and "Art as a Hermeneutic of Narrative," *The Center for Hermeneutical Studies in Hellenistic and Modern Culture*, Protocol of the Twenty-Fourth Colloquy (Berkeley: Graduate Theological Union, 1976) 1–22.

15. Doug Adams, review of William Dyrness, *Visual Faith: Art, Theology, and Worship in Dialogue* (Grand Rapids: Baker Academic, 2001) in *Christian Century* 119 (September 2002) n.p.

human activity.[16] But with his discussion of Christo's *Umbrellas* (1991), Adams shifts more explicitly to his own perspective, which slides into the assumption of ultimate Truth, when he comments that this project "gave us a sense of sheltering under God's providence."[17] Not surprisingly, this review was for a publication where this type of interpretation would be understood, if not expected.

By contrast, in the conclusion to his own book, Adams offers a more ecumenical, accessible perspective, stating that artworks such as those produced by Christo and Jean-Claude "help us perceive not only connections but also transcendent relations which lead us to center beyond ourselves and to sense not only our time and our place but also other generations and the earth beyond our place and time."[18] Adams is one of a few Christian scholars who successfully maintain a critical distance on faith, art, and the relationship between them. For the majority of religious scholars, any intrinsic value in art is secondary to a life understood in terms of, and lived according to, Christian tenets. To the non-believer, this is an extreme form of subjectivity that undermines rational enquiry, and therefore best left unmentioned, even in its absence. Thus, while a confession of the personal investment of the author in their subject matter has become a standard part of the art-historical study, it is still taboo to reference one's specific spiritual beliefs or general perspective on religion in this context.

At the same time, however, there are many contemporary works of art that suggest religious themes or reference Christian subject matter without promoting a specific agenda. The spiritual meaning of this type of art is usually recognized, but not addressed, because it is not literal or dogmatic, and therefore does not seem to belong to either the secular or religious realm. Indeed, its allusiveness is more compatible with theologies that

16. Ibid.

17. Ibid.

18. Doug Adams, *Transcendence with the Human Body in Art* (New York: Crossroad, 1991) 148.

are founded on metaphor, more open to doubt, to individual interpretation, and thus, to the more casual, partial referencing of the cultural, rather than practicing, Christian viewer.

In *The Body of God: An Ecological Theology*, Sallie McFague describes five major models within the Christian tradition for understanding the relationship between God and the world that are still familiar to western audiences today, even if they are non-believers. The impersonal deistic model sees God as the original creator of the world and its laws, which he is now separated from, except for perhaps in extreme crisis. By contrast, in the more intimate, dialogic model God's relationship is with the individual alone, with an emphasis on human sin and divine forgiveness. Within the monarchical model, God is the omnipotent king and believers are his obedient subjects, and in the agential model he is a type of super being whose intentions are realized in the world through the actions of humanity.[19] McFague's Process Theology proposes an organic model, where the universe, or world, is equated with God. Here the concept of human agency reflecting the presence of the divine is combined with the idea that all created agents—human and otherwise—are interdependent, with the divine being having preeminence. McFague posits a unifying Christian metaphor: the world as the body of God, a radicalization of divine transcendence and immanence that is not pantheism—where the world is equivalent to the divine—but panentheism, where God is in all aspects of the world but is not exhausted by it.[20] Here the Trinitarian concept of God the Father is replaced by a God who is both Creator and Creation.

Mark Wallace's "postmodern green theology" also finds the Creator Spirit in Nature—he describes God as "Earth Spirit, the compassionate, all-encompassing divine force within the biosphere who inhabits the earth community and continually works to maintain the integrity of all life forms."[21] In his review of

19. Sallie McFague, *The Body of God* (Minneapolis: Fortress, 1993) 137–41.

20. Ibid., 141.

21. Mark I. Wallace, *Finding God in the Singing River* (Minneapolis: Fortress, 2005) 6.

Wallace's book, *Finding God in the Singing River*, T. R. Thompson asks, from a perspective more concerned with biblical orthodoxy: "In Trinitarian terms, where are Father and Son personally and agentially in relation to the Spirit?"[22] This theological question is not important from a secular art-historical perspective; nor is it relevant for the many viewers who are aware of Christianity, and perhaps even raised with a version of its orthodoxy, but not committed to any ideological position, and not possessing a detailed knowledge of its symbolism.

The idea of the divine as, and in, Creation is not difficult to locate in the contemporary visual arts. Although her last works date to the mid-twentieth century, Emily Carr continues to be one of Canada's most prominent artists, and she is a particularly interesting example here because although her Christian beliefs, and her attempts to find the God of Creation in the natural world, are widely known from her published journals, they are rarely used to interpret her art.

Carr grew up in a religious family, and retained a lifelong aversion to the rigid, Victorian Christianity of her youth.[23] She experimented with other faiths, including, most famously, Theosophy, which she initially embraced under the influence of Lawren Harris, but eventually rejected completely, returning to a more personal version of Christianity.[24] Carr's explicit references to her relationship with God are usually not considered in the analysis of her paintings—probably because, as Doris Shadbolt admits, these passages use a religious terminology "that mesh(es) uncomfortably with our twentieth-centuries sensibilities."[25]

22. T. R. Thompson, review of *Finding God in the Singing River* (Minneapolis: Fortress, 2005), *Theology Today* 63 (2006) n.p.

23. Ann Davis, "Emily Carr's Mystic Soul," *The Literary Review of Canada* (February 1993) 11.

24. In a letter dated November 16, 1936, to her friend Edythe Hembroff-Schleicher, Carr writes about the "wuzzy theosophical point of view," adding: "I cannot see any justification for their beliefs. They are so vague, so vapid . . ." British Columbia Archives, Victoria.

25. Doris Shadbolt, *The Art of Emily Carr* (Vancouver, BC: Douglas & MacIntyre, 1979) 196.

Instead, Carr is typically characterized as a more generic mystic whose primarily spiritual goal was an unmediated communion with the divine.[26]

But Carr was a devout, if non-traditional, Christian, deeply concerned with feeling and communicating her love of God, and not shy about discussing in her journals the essential role religion played in her life. She wrote: "I believe it to be true that there is no true art without religion."[27] Her own faith, though idiosyncratic, retained the basic Trinitarian elements of Christianity. She writes about her relationship with Jesus and laments her inability to follow his example even as she chronicles at length her arguments with, and disapproval of, family and friends.[28] More important to her painting, however, was her belief in God and the sacredness of the natural world that was his Creation.[29]

Although her primary aim for her painting was to express this sacred presence, Carr eschewed explicit religious symbolism in favor of images that were more subtle and universal. This was no doubt an important factor in her eventual widespread acceptance in the Canadian art world, but it has also resulted in a disconnect between her artistic intentions with respect to her religion, and her critical reception. Carr's 1935 work, *Scorned as Timber, Beloved of the Sky*, for example, is seen as a representation of spar trees which are used as anchors to hoist logs. Chosen for their inner strength, spar trees were stripped of their lower branches, and often cut off completed at the top.[30] These

26. See for example, Ann Davis, *The Logic of Ecstasy: Canadian Mystical Painting 1920–1940* (Toronto: University of Toronto, 1992).

27. *The Complete Writings of Emily Carr* (Vancouver: Douglas & MacIntyre, 1997) 683.

28. Two of many examples of Carr's personal clashes are colorfully recounted in *Opposite Contraries: The Unknown Journals of Emily Carr and Other Writings*, Susan Crean, ed. (Vancouver, BC: Douglas & MacIntyre, 2004) 83–85. In the same volume, see 59–62, 64, for examples of her thoughts on Christ.

29. See especially the latter section of "Hundreds and Thousands," in *The Complete Writings of Emily Carr*, as in n. 28.

30. Exhibition label, *Emily Carr: New Perspectives on a Canadian Icon,*

three have survived the devastation of clear cutting, and though maimed below, their upward reach is seemingly limitless. Behind them a swirling, dazzling, otherworldly light, energy, and space, open up. The recent major Carr exhibition described this vital force as "the churning breath of life," which the artist interpreted through animism and anthropomorphism.[31] It did not note the number of spindly trees, which is likely a reference to the three crosses on Golgotha. The tallest tree, much larger and in the foreground, is stripped of its foliage closer to the earthly plane, but verdant with life at its upper reaches where it communes with the heavens. Scorned as timber, the least of the trees—mutilated but still possessed of an inner beauty—are those that strive to reach beyond their mere physical existence.

These elements can be understood as a symbolic self portrait of a woman, isolated and misunderstood, whose manner, appearance and living situation did not conform to the standards of the provincial city of Victoria, and who found comfort in the church, her own reading of the Bible, and most of all, in the presence, in the natural world, of the Creator God to whom she felt beloved.[32]

Within Process Theology there is also a less dogmatic formulation of that other part of the Trinity known as the Holy Spirit, which traditionally focused on human beings and on the followers of Christ in particular, as the "divine wind" from Genesis. This is a complex and varying metaphor for the source of life for the universe, one that McFague argues is necessarily a *back*, not *face*

Vancouver Art Gallery, 2007, exhibition catalogue (Vancouver, BC: Douglas & MacIntyre, 2006).

31. Ibid.

32. For a short but representative glimpse of Carr's personality see the chapter on the artist in Mary Ann Caws, *Glorious Eccentrics: Modernist Women Painting and Writing* (New York: Palgrave, 2006). A extensive analysis of the breadth of Carr's beliefs and artistic practice that gives some consideration to her religion is provided in Stephanie Kirkwood Walker, *This Woman in Particular: Contexts for the Biographical Image of Emily Carr* (Ottawa: Wilfred Laurier Press, 1996).

term: it alludes to something that by its very nature cannot be precisely described. This is God as "spirit," present in inanimate forms, making the ordinary sacred and numinous—sometimes referred to as the sanctifying God.[33]

Although Carr herself wrote of the difficulty of explaining the spirit, *Dancing Sunlight* (c. 1937–40) and *A Rushing Sea of Undergrowth* (1935), are only two of her many paintings that correspond to her belief that this force could be suggested in visual form, if not represented precisely.[34] Here Carr represents the spirit within the growth and movement of the British Columbia forest, demonstrating her belief that "our mistake is trying to humanize the woods to make them conform to us, instead of going out to them in a spirit of recognition of the God spirit among them."[35]

Mary Pratt is another prominent Canadian artist who references the Christian faith, but in a different manner. Though Pratt is averse to speaking at length about the meaning of her work, she willingly provides biographical and anecdotal contexts for her art, which include her religious upbringing and continued belief in the presence of God.[36] On the connection between her early desire for God to reveal Himself to her, and her later choice of profession, she comments: "Maybe that longing to be shown the world helped me later when the world did show itself visually to me."[37] And considering the human propensity to build churches, "places in which one can trap and keep the idea of God," she

33. This is similar to Tillich's concept of "sacramental art"; see "Art and Ultimate Reality," *Art, Creativity, and the Sacred: An Anthology in Religion and Art*, Diane Apostolos-Cappadona, ed. (New York: Continuum, 1995), 219–35.

34. *The Complete Writings of Emily Carr*, 675.

35. Ibid., 761.

36. On Pratt's current religious life and its relation to her art see Gerta Moray, *Mary Pratt* (Toronto: McGraw-Hill Ryerson, 1989), 32. Another perspective on her biography is provided by Tom Smart, *The Art of Mary Pratt: The Substance of Light* (Fredericton: Goose Lane, 1995).

37. Robin Laurence, "The Radiant Way," *Canadian Art* 11 (1994) 30.

wonders, "Is this the best way to find God? Or is it better to keep your eyes open than to keep your hands busy?"[38]

Pratt paints many subjects with a long history as Christian symbols, including fish, suppers, fire, bathing, but she does not paint religious subjects, preferring broad themes associated with the faith instead. Her *Christmas Fire* (1981) uses the traditional metaphor of the fire of the Holy Spirit, suggesting its connection to the birth of the Christian messiah without losing her emphasis on the power of the domestic experience of the natural element. Pratt also focuses our attention on the sacred in what might otherwise be mundane—the shimmering blues and red flames, the rising ash, and heat against the winter's night.

Most of Pratt's intensely, hyper-realistic, studies of the ordinary can be read in a similar manner, but certain subjects prompt a particularly Christian reflection on numinosity. Though beautiful in themselves, *Pomegranates in a Crystal Bowl* (1984), is also, by way of the myth of Persephone, a reference to Resurrection. In *Red Currant Jelly* (1972) and similar works, Pratt's exquisitely painted jars intensify the presence of this very ordinary substance, and of the otherworldly light which illuminates it—in her own words: "because jelly is so beautiful—such a clear and brilliant reminder of its origins—we treat it with the respect given to the major symbols in our culture."[39] *Jellies for Thanksgiving* (1994), sit "in a scattered line, emerging from the dark background, their elliptical surfaces catching brilliant light, soft in focus, their dark interiors glowing from an unseen light source."[40]

Pratt's intensely-focused naturalism both validates and denies traditional Christian imagery—her pomegranates and jelly are meant to be eaten, but they are also presented as objects for contemplation. Some viewers might be aware of their having a traditional Christian meaning, but the artist is subtle in her

38. Mary Pratt, *A Personal Calligraphy* (Fredericton: Goose Lane, 2000), 102.

39. Moray, *Mary Pratt*, 58.

40. Ibid., 113.

encouragement of this reading. The vivid red suggests, but does not represent, the Christian Eucharist. These everyday items are rooted firmly in personal experience, suggesting that faith itself belongs to this realm. Though she does not espouse any particular doctrine, her images are consistent with Feminist Theology that validates the lived experience of women against the patriarchal tradition of absolutes.[41]

In orthodox Christianity the second part of the Trinity, the Son, "the only begotten of the Father" (John 1:14), is cited by many Christian scholars as a validation of artistic creativity. Trevor Hart, for example, states that "recognition that, in Jesus, God's own Word has taken flesh and dwelt among us humanly clearly raises difficulty for any denigration of the physical in accounts of artistic meaning and creativity";[42] a similar argument is made for art as an echo of divine creativity.[43] A more radical view of the incarnation endorses the concept of "degree Christology"—where Jesus is understood as different in degree not in kind, as a paradigm, not an enigma; a culmination of the enfleshment of the divine.[44] Here not just images of the humanity and divinity of Jesus, but any reference to divine creative power, or to the sacredness of Creation itself in human terms, can allude to Incarnation. Andy Goldsworthy's continued emphasis on the role of the artist in the creation of the work—in *Broken Pebbles* (1985) and *Broken Icicle* (1986), for example—avoids mere narcissism with a vision directed beyond himself to the natural world;

41. See Rebecca Chopp, "Feminism's Theological Pragmatics: A Social Naturalism of Women's Experience," *The Journal of Religion* 67 (1987) 239–56; and Richard Grigg, "Enacting the Divine: Feminist Theology and the Being of God," *Journal of Religion* 74 (1994) 506–23.

42. Trevor Hart, "Through the Arts: Hearing, Seeing and Touching the Truth," *Beholding the Glory: Incarnation though the Arts* (Grand Rapids: Baker, 2000).

43. This is discussed in chapter 11 of Hilary Brand and Adrienne Chaplin, *Art and Soul: Signposts for Christianity in the Arts* (Carlisle, UK: Solway, 1999).

44. McFague, *The Body of God*, 133.

but while he has been characterized as a "card-carrying man of the soul,"[45] Goldsworthy's own written and verbal accounts do little to encourage a deeper reading of his work. Nevertheless, his meditative, almost sacramental interaction with form and process, suggests a spiritual element: a human emulation, and incarnation, of the divine force, enacting and representing the transient, yet eternal, beauty of creation.[46]

Joshua Taylor refers to this as a "communitive" type of art—which he declares, "never allow[s] us to forget we are members of a physical race by referencing the bodily presence of the artist and the viewer through indexicality."[47] The contrast between this spiritual interpretation and the narrower traditional Christian ideology is illustrated once again by Doug Adams, who, in discussing Taylor's theories, states: "realizing oneself to be a finite creature with limited capabilities is a corollary of acknowledging God to be Creator and Christ to be Judge and Redeemer."[48]

Many Christians writing on the arts consider the contemporary versions of traditional imagery associated with incarnation—for example, the portrait of Jesus referenced earlier—to be now "trivialized," pale imitations of a popular culture in decline.[49] But there are many recent examples of figures with Christ-like qualities who are not otherwise religious. The most well known is probably Neo in *The Matrix*—a film that is more subtle in its Christian themes than its Christian referents.[50] Less promi-

45. David Lee, "In Profile: Goldsworthy," *Art Review* (February 1995) 6.

46. Andy Goldsworthy, *A Collaboration with Nature* (New York: Abrams, 1990); Thomas Riedelsheimer et al., *Rivers and Tides: Andy Goldsworthy Working with Time*, videorecording, (Burlington, VT: Docurama, 2004).

47. Cited in Doug Adams, "Theological Expressions through Visual Art Forms," in *Art, Creativity, and the Sacred*, Diane Apostolos-Cappadona, ed. (New York: Continuum, 1995) 313.

48. Adams, *Transcendence with the Human Body in Art*, 315.

49. See Gregory Wolfe, *Intruding Upon the Timeless: Meditations on Art, Faith, and Mystery*, (Baltimore: Square Halo, 2003) 48–50.

50. See Angela Ndalianis, "Caravaggio Reloaded: Neo-baroque Poetics," *Caravaggio and His World: Darkness and Light* (Sydney: Art Gallery of New

nent in North America, but at the forefront of visual culture in Britain, are the new series of *Dr. Who*, and its spinoff, *Torchwood*, which use multiple Christian referents in their exploration of moral and metaphysical themes. They are often seen as either an endorsement or indictment of Christianity, but only according to a fundamentalist version of the faith.[51] Their emphasis on metaphorical concepts rather than literal truths can be seen as a more flexible concept of the Christian deity that encourages the interested viewer to understand how these and other examples of contemporary visual culture might allude to creation, the divine within humanity, or the presence of the spirit, without demanding that they subscribe to a given doctrine or that ultimately, they even believe in the "God" posited by this or any other Christian theology.

South Wales; Melbourne: National Gallery of Victoria, 2003) 72–76.

51. For example, the *Doctor Who* episode "Gridlock" was nominated for an Epiphany prize (www.templeton.org/prizes/), awarded to programs that "help increase man's understanding and love of God." Previous television winners— *Seventh Heaven* and *Doc*—were explicitly Christian, where *Doctor Who* is not.

7

Visual Culture and the Sacred

Creative Acts of Resistance and Redemption in Art, Film, and New Media

Scott Parsons *and* David O'Hara

INTRODUCTION: PEIRCE'S MYSTICAL EXPERIENCE AND THE VISUAL

IN AN UNPUBLISHED LETTER written in the late nineteenth century, the philosopher and semiotician Charles Peirce wrote to the Episcopal bishop of New York to tell the bishop of an experience he had recently had in a New York City church. Peirce writes that he had stopped in the church to look at the chancel, as he occasionally would do. This time, however, as he gazed at the chancel, he felt he "received the master's permission to approach the altar" and receive communion. Peirce was not observantly religious before this, nor was he particularly so afterwards. He concluded his letter by saying that he had never before been mystical, but that he now was. In good mystical form, he does not explain what he means by this.[1]

1. The letter is dated "1892 April 24." A copy of it may be found in the archives of the Institute of American Thought at IUPUI in Indianapolis.

Let us make just two brief observations about Peirce's letter: First, he makes a strong connection between the visual sign of the sacred and his mystical experience. We usually expect logicians to justify their beliefs propositionally and logically, but the only explanation Peirce gives for this mysticism is that he first looked at some liturgical art.

Our second observation is this: his mysticism does not lead him to what we might consider a typical life of religious devotion. We don't have records of him spending long periods in prayer, or attending mass, or engaging in works of service. Nevertheless, his writings for the rest of his life express a peculiar concern for the importance of religion for every aspect of life. In other words, his mysticism doesn't just lead him to particular religious acts; rather, it seems to have led him to see ubiquitous connections between the sacred and the ordinary. What began in the sacred space of the chancel wound up moving seamlessly into the rest of the world.

CONTEXT: OUR CAPSTONE CLASS AT AUGUSTANA— FINDING THE SACRED ON THE PRAIRIE

This story has particular relevance for us because of the way it speaks to a class we teach together at Augustana College, a college affiliated with the Evangelical Lutheran Church in America in Sioux Falls, South Dakota. Before graduating from Augustana, every senior must complete what we call a "Capstone" course, the purpose of which is to provoke students to reflect in an ethical manner on the whole of their education and subsequently to ask "how then shall we live?" These classes are taught by faculty from across the disciplines, and aim to integrate learning from several fields. We teach one of these Capstone classes, entitled "Visual Culture and the Sacred-Creative Acts of Resistance and Redemption in Art, Film and New Media." Our aim in teaching it is to help our students to consider and engage with the importance of the visual and its relation to the sacred.

Seeking the sacred outside of traditional liturgical settings can be a slightly tricky proposition at a church-related college. Although our Midwestern students come from a variety of religious traditions, they have imbibed respect for traditional religion with mother's milk. That respect is powerful enough that at times it can trump what they might otherwise believe or perceive. Certain tokens and signs of the sacred are stamped in the level prairie consciousness of South Dakota and stand in starker relief than a rural Lutheran steeple rising out of a treeless plain. The steeples of the prairie are beautiful: they rise out of a lonely place and remind us we are not alone; they call us together to sing and to gaze at leaded stained-glass windows; they tell us that even on the still unpopulated frontier the Holy has gone before us and met us. But they can also have the effect of insulating the sacred and of making us suspect that the sacred lies only behind heavy oak doors, only in isolated boxes of pews, or only high and out of reach, somewhere transcendent in that place to which the steeple points.

There is a kind of irony, of course, in doing this work among Lutherans. The Reformation began as an attempt to disrupt the deadening violence of absolute mediation, and it gave us a new freedom to seek the sacred in its immediacy. Nonetheless Lutheranism is not exempt from the general rule that when religious life becomes routine, it runs the unintended risk, despite its very beautiful forms of worship, of leading its adherents to assume that it is only in the mediation of those forms that the sacred may be approached. Many of our students have grown up in churches and already have fixed habits of understanding the relationship between the visual and the sacred. (Ironically, some of these habits run counter to the established theological traditions in which they have grown up.) The sacred can show up in certain signs, but context and culture wind up conditioning and limiting those signs. Our students are probably like many of their contemporaries in this: for many of our students, crosses, altars, chancels, *ichthus*-fish, steeples, stained glass saints, and other similar signs denote the sacred, and those things without liturgical significance do not. Furthermore, in general, our students are not aware of just how those signs came to portray or indicate the sacred. Ordinary objects are made sacred by being inscribed with those liturgical symbols or by being placed in liturgical spaces. We are reminded of the story of the Sunday-school teacher who holds up a picture of a carrot and asks her class what it is. After a long and uncomfortable silence, one timid child finally ventures, "well, it looks like a carrot, but since this is church, I'll say it's Jesus." The carrot is profane but the context stamps it as religious. But is it possible for such a picture to speak of the sacred in any other way? Are the sacred and the profane so plainly and merely differentiated by some outward tokens or by the space in which they are seen?

In teaching our class, we begin by assuming that there is in fact some relation between what matters most in our lives and the sacred. To some degree, this is admittedly informed by our own religious culture—we were raised as a Lutheran and an Episcopalian—but we also think it is a reasonable assumption for any religious standpoint. If the sacred is insulated from some part of the profane then it is, to that degree, irrelevant for our lives. While we want our students to consider the relation of the visual to the sacred, we do not want them to make the quick equation of their customary representations of the sacred to the sacred. In other words, there are more things that matter in our lives than those things that happen on Sundays or in plainly religious contexts. Couldn't it be that the sacred touches those things too? And if so, might it not show up in the visual? To borrow from the traditional language used to describe sacraments, might there not be some "outward and visible sign" of this "inward and spiritual grace?"

In practical terms, our course attempts to combine history, theory, and practice in a way that gets art- and mostly non-art majors enthusiastically engaged in producing and thinking about the role of art in their pursuit of what matters most in their lives, and to get people from diverse religious traditions engaged in conversation about the numinous and the transcendent apart from dogma. In what follows we will try to tell—and show— you how we try to do that.

Our course is by no means perfect! Naturally, we approach this class from our areas of expertise, drawing on our respective strengths as a studio arts professor and public artist, on the one hand, and as a philosopher with an interest in history and theology on the other hand. But we also approach this class as students, learning from one another and from the students as well. We do not want simply to tell the students what we know; we want to show them how we learn. Not surprisingly, we learn through a combination of studying the history and theory of both the visual and the sacred, and the practice of trying to engage the sacred through our own creative work.

HISTORY AND THEORY: LEARNING TO READ

We can summarize our approach to the course by calling to mind another word from Peirce: "Truly to paint the ground where we ourselves are standing is an impossible problem in historical perspective."[2] Peirce, like Hegel before him and Foucault after him, reminds us that the regulative concepts that so strongly affect us are often opaque to us except through historical examination. For example, while many of our Protestant students "know" that they should not venerate icons, most do not know why this is so, nor even what is meant by an icon. By supplying our students with readings in theological aesthetics sampled from across the last three thousand years, we introduce them to their heritage and try to show them some of the ways in which we have intentionally attended to the importance of the visual in the Western Christian traditions. This turns out to be a more powerful facet of our course than we anticipated when we designed the course. Many of our students are at least familiar with the Biblical injunction

2. C. Hartshorne, P. Weiss, and A. Burks, eds., *Collected Papers of Charles Sanders Peirce* (Cambridge: Harvard University Press, 1935, 1958) 4.32.

against making graven images. Nevertheless, that commandment strikes them as irrelevant for our times, so they do not tend to notice the other things their tradition says about the importance of the visual, like the instructions Moses receives about the way that the Ark of the Covenant and the Tabernacle must *look*. It is as though many churches today have taken the commandment against graven images as a dismissal of all visual art. The descriptions of the Ark and Tabernacle, on the other hand, affirm Peirce's point that the visual may be at least as anagogical as texts.

What the historical readings and discussions do for us is to help the students see that while they cannot simply paint the ground they stand upon, they can at least trace the steps that have brought them to where they stand. More importantly, it shows them that they need not be merely passive recipients of a tradition, especially if part of that tradition is itself an invitation to an active engagement with re-examining the visual.

One difficulty in teaching a class like this to non-artist students is in choosing the readings. We opted to compile readings that approached visual culture from a range of perspectives. They included a variety of religious, historical, and theoretical texts, as well as a number of short pieces by and about contemporary artists and art theorists, including Andrei Codrescu, Donald Kuspit, John Berger, Makoto Fujimura, Deborah Haynes, Stephen Nachmanovitch, Wassily Kandinsky, Walter Benjamin, Ron Burnett, and Susan Sontag.

If you were to poll our students and ask them which were the most helpful texts, we doubt there would be much consensus. Each student found resonances with different texts. A small handful of our more conservative religious students found Francis Schaeffer's *Art and the Bible* to be an eye-opening text. We should emphasize this "small handful" since many of our students found Schaeffer to be of limited value. Its perspective is admittedly narrow, but it served an important role in our class. Schaeffer's somewhat dismissive overture to visual art is to allow that it can in some ways offer a distant approximation to biblical truth and to the human condition. This can come across as being a little like saying that psychology offers some distant approximations to the proper way to frame a house; while it may be true, it's a failure to appreciate psychology or art for their own sake or on their own terms. Nevertheless, for that handful of students Schaeffer was a helpful addition since he helped them to see that art and religion do not need to be at odds with one another. For those who grow up in an anaesthetic or visually anhedonic religious tradition, Schaeffer's book can be like an inviting doorway into a new world of appreciating visual culture.

Schaeffer points out to contemporary Christians that the Bible contains vivid and important descriptions of visual art, each of which is explicitly connected to Jewish or Christian worship. Some religious traditions place a good deal of weight on the commandment against graven images. Other passages, especially in the Christian Scriptures, suggest that what is seen is unimportant or irrelevant. For example, in chapter thirteen of the Gospel of Mark, Jesus' disciples call his attention to the magnificence of the stones used to build the Temple. Jesus' reply that "all these stones will be thrown down" could be taken as a Christian dismissal of religious art. Similarly there are those passages in St Paul's Epistles to the Romans (ch. 8) and to the Corinthians (I Corinthians 13) that strongly prefer the not-yet-visible over the visible. And St. John, in his first Epistle, cautioned Christians against succumbing to "the desire of the eyes" (I John 2:16) and ended his epistle with the words, "Children, protect yourselves from images."[3]

Schaeffer points out that passages like these, which are very few in number, must be read in the light of the numerous biblical texts that show the goodness of the visual. Significantly, Schaeffer points to those passages where God commands Israel to construct the very Temple Jesus' disciples admired. In such passages[4] it is

---

3. Or "idols"—the Greek word is *eidolon*, which can be translated "image or "idol." Our translation.

4. Schaeffer points to Exodus 25:9 as an example of divine mandate for

apparent that both representational art and art for beauty's sake are taken to be essential to proper worship. Even St. John is not so plainly opposed to seeing as it might seem at first. After all, he begins his epistle by declaring not just once but twice that what he is proclaiming as the Gospel is what he and the other disciples *have seen with their eyes;*[5] and he says a little later on that one aim of holy love is that it moves us from darkness into light and ends our blindness.[6] However these words may be understood, they plainly cannot be taken simply to diminish the importance of the visual! Anyone who, like Peirce in 1892, has stood in reverential awe before a breathtaking canvas or chancel already knows the power of art to move some kind of spiritual response, but we must remember that some traditions are suspicious of such responses. The value of Schaeffer's book was that it allowed the students from such traditions to see that the very texts they took to validate their suspicions actually urge them to connect visual culture and the sacred. As professors, we could simply have demanded that our students put aside their prejudices and study the rest of our texts with us, but this struck us as too ungentle an approach, especially with so much at stake. How ironic it would have been had we tried to strong-arm our students into seeing how delicate art can be.

Michel Foucault and Peirce have both argued that the ideas that shape our inner life are often cultural artifacts concerning whose provenance we are largely ignorant.[7] Peirce liked to quote Shakespeare's *Measure for Measure* in defense of this point: "proud man / Most ignorant of what he's most assured / His glassy essence."[8] More prosaically, Peirce argued that we think in signs

---

visual design; and to passages like 1 Chronicles 28:11–12 and 2 Chronicles 3–4 as examples of how this was carried out.

5. 1 John 1:1, 3.

6. 1 John 2:8–11.

7. See the first chapter of Foucault's *Discipline and Punish*, for example.

8. Act II, scene 2, lines 117–20. Cf. Peirce's "Some Consequences of Four Incapacities," written in 1868, and his "Man's Glassy Essence," written in 1892. Both are in *The Essential Peirce I* (Bloomington: Indiana University Press, 1992).

and that we *are* signs, but we rarely reflect consciously on those signs that constitute us. So studying the history of ideas and signs and art is like doing intellectual anatomical exercises. If Peirce is right, it's surprising that churches do so little to teach their congregants the history of Christian art. With the exception of some of our religion majors, most of our students know very little about Christian history despite its deep influence on their culture. One set of our readings is intended to familiarize our students with some of the controversies that lie half-asleep in the dark corners of the history of Christian thought. When we first taught our class, Gesa Elsbeth Thiessen had recently published a helpful anthology called *Theological Aesthetics* (Grand Rapids: Eerdmans, 2004). Using that as our sourcebook, we invited our students to journey back through the tense history of Christian argumentation about visual culture. From its earliest years, Christianity has been stretched between the poles of immanence and transcendence, between attention to the present world and devotion to the world to come. St Paul writes that "Now remain these three things: faith, hope, and love. But the greatest of these is love."[9] If the greatest, love, is attentive to the beloved world, nevertheless the other two, faith and hope, seem to point to the world that is not yet.[10] Some early Christian theologians worshiped God as the divine artist or found kinship between Christian theology and Plato's idea that there is a divine demiurge.[11] This justified ap-

---

9. 1 Corinthians 13:1; our translation.

10. Gregory Wolfe has commented helpfully on this tension between immanent love and transcendent faith and their relation to art in an editorial in *Image*: "Faith, according to the letter to the Hebrews, is 'the substance of things hoped for.' That phrasing, from the King James Version, hasn't been improved upon in recent translations. In faith, what is hoped for becomes present, substantial. To live in faith means to live in the present, to know that the substance of grace is here and now. That is not to say that faith involves some sort of simple possession; it is, rather, to exists in the tension between the presence we encounter and the sense of what that presence means for our destiny . . . Faith, far from making us apathetic, enables us to be present to what surrounds us." *Image* 62 (Summer 2009).

11. This idea occurs in several places in Plato's writing, but notably in his

preciation of beauty wherever it occurs in the world. Such appreciation may not seem to need justification, but other Christians, emphasizing the commandment against idolatry, argued that the work of craftsmen and artists only distracted the Christian from the true object of worship. For instance, Justin Martyr urged Christians to cultivate an abstract intellectual worship without the use of images, and the apologist Lactantius argued that material objects lacked real life and so were poor substitutes for the living God. In the tradition of apophatic theology we have figures like Gregory of Nyssa who declare that truly "seeing [god] is to be found in not seeing," apparently diminishing the importance of visual culture for theology.[12]

In the older traditions of Roman Catholicism and Eastern Orthodoxy the issue came to some conclusion after the Second Council of Nicaea (787), where, in a way, the issue was settled by appeal to the doctrine of Incarnation: to insist that God cannot be represented in matter is to deny the possibility of the Incarnation;[13] but Christians cannot consistently deny this doctrine; so matter must be able to represent the divine. Of course, this does not completely resolve the issue, but it allows the discussion to turn towards finer distinctions like the difference between *worship* of images and *veneration* of images; and the difference between seeing God *in* or *as* images and seeing God *through* images as one sees through a window or through a story. Of course theory and practice travel at different speeds and often on different paths. No doubt Christians continued to maintain a variety of attitudes and practices concerning visual art, and some of the disputes simmered under the surface. But these disputes produced a record

---

Timaeus (e.g., 28a) and *Republic* (e.g., 596–99). The word "demiurge" means something like "(public) craftsman" or even "creator."

12. Gregory of Nyssa, *Life of Moses*, 163. Cited in Richard Kearney, "Desire of God," in *God, the Gift, and Postmodernism*, John D. Caputo and Michael J. Scanlon, eds. (Bloomington: Indiana University Press, 1999) 139. Of course, Nyssa is speaking of how Moses "saw" God by seeing God's effects, which is arguably a reason to attend to the appearance of the sacred in the profane.

13. Theodore of Studio (759–826) offers a similar defense of icons.

in words and images that our students came to learn to read and interpret.

Perhaps the teacher's greatest reward when going through a review of ancient history comes at that moment when the students begin to see that this is not *just* ancient history but, in some very real sense, the history of what we believe right now. *De nobis fabula narratur*, we could say; the story that is told is told *about us*. As our historical readings progressed through Luther and Bonhoeffer and Chittister, our students began to see more clearly how much of their visual hermeneutic is inherited, and just what that heritage is.

One breakthrough moment came when we were looking at our college's seal. The seal bears a triangle inscribed in a circle. Inside the triangle is an open book with the letters VDMA. The book is divided by a *stauron* that rises above it, and an oil lamp burns below it. To the right and left of the book are the letters *alpha* and *omega*. Our students must pass by this seal a dozen times a day around our campus, but few bother to *see* it or to read it. We spent a little time talking about the letters. The *alpha* and *omega* are obvious enough. VDMA stands for *Verbum Dei Manet [in] Aeternum* (from Isaiah 40:6–8 and I Peter 1:25, "the word of God lasts forever"). Then we asked the class what they knew of the symbol that bisected the open book. Most recognized that is was a cross of some sort (that is what *stauron* means, after all) but were unsure why it looked like it had the letter "P" inscribed over it. The *stauron* is scribal shorthand for "Christ," and is a variant of the *chi-rho* symbol made by inscribing a *rho* over a *chi* (the *chi-rho* looks like an "X" written on top of a "P"). It was a way of saving pen strokes since it abbreviates the name "Christ" to just its first two letters (*chi* and *rho* in the Greek word *Christos*). The *stauron* simply takes the *chi* and turns it forty-five degrees so it makes a cross + rather than an "X". The *rho* then looks like a man's head leaning to the side, perhaps in agony on the cross. What began as an abbreviation became a picture, a miniature theology in layers of signs. Of course these signs can be seen in many churches on altars, in chancels, and on stained glass windows, but many of our students have grown up in a visually illiterate religious culture and have not learned to read those signs.

When we discovered this, our class took a new direction, since we realized that our students were surrounded by symbols that they knew to be somehow religious but which they had never learned to read. So we began to teach them about the symbolism of icons and their place in Christian liturgy. In one class, we projected an image of an icon of *Jesus Pantokrator* and talked about the position of the fingers of Jesus' right hand. Many of our students told us later that they had thought of such images as boring examples of poor representational art. Yes, they had seen the funny hand-position before, but had never known that with his fingers he is making four letters—the Greek letters IC XC, an abbreviation of *Iêsous Christos*—while blessing the one viewing the icon. In the icon, word and image merge into one richly layered sign, and that sign becomes a window through which we can see the history and theology of the church—and arguably the Divine as well.

In some sense all of these historical and theological readings are prologue to what will be (to our readers) much more familiar texts, like Kandinsky's *Concerning the Spiritual in Art*, or texts by Berger, Collingwood, Kant, or Langer. We won't dwell on our students' reactions to those texts. Let it suffice to say that the combination of readings about art with daily practices of creating art and with discussions about the development of traditions of visual culture helped our students to begin to see themselves. Had we asked them beforehand if they knew the college seal or recognized the figure of Jesus in icons, most might have said they did. But recognition of the images is not the same as understanding what those images are doing, how they are participating in human thought about the sacred.

We are reminded of Jacques Derrida's words: "We cannot be sure that we are not hallucinating simply by saying 'I see' ('I see' is, after all, just what the hallucinating person says). No, in order to check that you are not hallucinating you have to read in a certain way. I have no rule for that."[14] The trick in teaching is often figuring out how to help students "read in a certain way." Derrida is right: there is no rule for this. It has to be done with careful attention to the particulars, just as surely as reading cannot be done well without paying attention to the particular words.

One of our readings, Ron Burnett's *How Images Think*, attempts to address this problem of how one learns to see and read and think with images.

> *Seeing* is an activity of creative engagement with processes of *thinking* and *feeling* . . . Seeing and thinking have been bundled into reductive notions of perception as if perception were somehow less mediated and more instantaneous than just gazing or looking . . . *If to see is to create,* then images are never "just" the product of one or many internal or external processes. The distance needed to understand "sight"—distance from an event, person, or picture—is created through an act of engagement that temporarily connects and overcomes the storm of thought within the human mind. Even familiarity with a scene may not provide enough information to make vantage point clear or usable for interpretive or experiential purposes.[15]

Today we are barraged by images; if all images were translated into sound, much of our world would be cacophony. Our students have grown up learning how to sort and judge images quickly. In some sense they were familiar with the images we showed them, but they needed help learning how to see and read them slowly and carefully.

Let us mention one other text—Susan Sontag's book *Regarding the Pain of Others*—which mattered quite a lot to our students. When they looked at explicitly religious texts and images, our

14. Jacques Derrida, in *Questioning Ethics*, ed. Richard Kearney and Mark Dooley (London: Routledge, 1998).

15. Ron Burnett, *How Images Think* (Cambridge, MA: MIT Press, 2004) 13.

students were fairly quick learners, readily coming to understand the relationship between the visual and the sacred. But some of the most profound moments came when our students began to grapple with the way the sacred is touched on in the horrific. Why should there be any place in the world, any image at all from which the sacred is excluded? There is no such exclusion; there is only a failure to see it.

In a way, this text—along with a number of accompanying images that we discussed—was transformative for a number of students. As Sontag puts it, "Certain photographs—emblems of suffering, such as the snapshot of the little boy in the Warsaw Ghetto in 1943, his hands raised, being herded to the transport to a death camp—can be used like memento mori, as objects of contemplation to deepen one's sense of reality; as secular icons, if you will."[16]

Apart from the ethical considerations that arise in both the taking and viewing of photographs that depict the suffering of the Other, Susan Sontag's book was instrumental in introducing the history of photography, the multiple, and its relationship to modernity and postmodernity. Her book reviews quite a number of pivotal photographs in the history of photography (her book itself has no images), and we discovered that many students were not familiar with a number of these images. After our discussion on Goya, we used etching needles on small plates of copper and printed them on a traditional intaglio press. We viewed daguerreotypes and contrasted this experience to contemporary snapshot portraiture and digital memory cards. We looked through a camera obscura and a nineteenth-century stereo viewer to think about how we interact with and construct images,[17] and we weighed assumptions and beliefs about the truth-telling of

16. Susan Sontag, *Regarding the Pain of Others* (New York: Picador, 2003) 119.

17. Perhaps quite famous at this point, Jonathan Crary traces the history of visuality in *Techniques of the Observer: On Vision and Modernity in the Nineteenth Century* (Cambridge, MA: MIT Press, 1990).

photography and the "fictional" photographs of Jeff Wall and the photographic narratives of Duane Michals.

We are sure that much of this is quite familiar territory for those reading this book, but we mention this as an illustration of how, for our class, theory and practice informed one another and helped our students to see that the visual culture that surrounds them is not fixed, eternal, unchanging and impassive. Rather, as Peirce would put it, signs shape us and we shape signs. As we asked this ethical question at the heart of our class, it became evident that one part of our answer to it must lie in knowledge, but another part must lie in action. That is, we must become more media-savvy, more literate, and more critical about the visual culture around us; but then we've got to do something with what we know.

PRACTICE: HOW THEN SHALL WE LIVE?

This brings us to the most important part of our class, and the part that pleases us the most: as our budding theorists began to theorize, they translated their theorizing into practice.

What we have sketched out here about learning to "read" images took place over a whole semester, of course. From our historical and theoretical discussions it was a short step to talking about liturgy. It is worth remembering that our word "liturgy" is derived from two Greek words meaning "public works/service" or even "what the people do." Theory and history are extremely important, but they really begin to be meaningful when they encounter practice. To extend our metaphor of reading, it was our hope not just to teach students to read visual culture; we wanted them to learn to be active participants in the shaping and making of their visual culture.

In the course of this class, we engage in more practices than we have space to discuss here. We think that's important: we make our students read a lot, write even more, and to get their hands and eyes very busy in their world. Every week we make our students work on seeing, on observing, and interacting with the visual. For now, we'll focus on four of these practices: Site Visits, our Image of the Day Club, our Sacred Line Project, and our One Minute Videos.

Site Visits

We often think about prayer as words, but when we pray we do things not just with words but with our bodies and our space as well. With this insight in mind, we sent our students out to spend some time dwelling on the visual and the sacred in a number of places. Our only rules were that some of those spaces be spaces they considered sacred and others were to be spaces they considered profane. The distinction between "place" and "space" is something we want to develop and allow our students to recognize and author. On these excursions, the requirement was simply to be in a space for a minimum of one hour and to draw, think, write, and ultimately make the space theirs, transforming the space into a place that held a relationship tethering memory and the present to themselves in that particular place or landscape.

This exercise was unfamiliar and uncomfortable for many of our students. Several of our nursing students remarked with some consternation that they were accustomed to very specific assignments that detailed what the task was, how it was to be completed, and what results to expect. The open-endedness of this assignment had a few of them squirming in their seats, and seeing their discomfort we were tempted to do something to set them more at ease. We resisted the temptation, however, because we did not want our conceptions of sacred or profane spaces to get in the way of their discoveries. No doubt some were concerned about how such an assignment would be graded, and along with that, how they would know when they had completed it to the teachers' satisfaction. Grading these assignments is admittedly more difficult than, say, a multiple-choice quiz, and giving such an assignment can be an act of faith on the part of the teacher, since we don't know what to expect either. In the end, most of our students were willing to give it an honest try, and the results were often remarkable. One nursing student visited and wrote about the rock pile on her parents' farm. Anyone who has grown up on a prairie farm knows about "picking rock" each year, gathering up the rocks that are plowed up and making piles of them off at the edges of the fields. Around such old piles tall grasses and groves will sometimes grow up. Our student sat on one such pile and wrote this:

> A grove is commonly known to hold junk and dilapidated items. However, since my early childhood, I have been fascinated with this space on my parents' farm. My dad stores many pieces of old rusty farm machinery in this area, there is even a large rotting portion of the house in which my dad grew up.
>
> As I sit on the rock pile, in case you're wondering it is a pile of rocks that I have picked from my dad's fields, I can see the sacredness all around me. The rocks I am sitting on represent my own physical labor. I have worked many grueling hours to assist in the natural growing process. I helped remove the rocks to help my dad's crops grow easier. I visualize this to be similar to picking the sins out of my life, to assist in the natural growing process for humans.
>
> The rusty machinery, rotting house, and molding trees resemble the life cycle. These things all had their moments of glory and have now transitioned into their retirement. They represent the natural life cycle that both objects and humans undergo. I find this cycle quite sacred. I have witnessed every stage of the life cycle in humans, including birth, toddlers progressing to school age children, adults, and elders up to their death.
>
> During the birth of a baby, it is difficult not to witness the sacred in this event. Many conditions have to align for the baby to be conceived and born, which is quite amazing. I directly relate this to the sacred presence of God. The dying process is even more sacred to me. Often, people miraculously improve in their condition immediately before dying. For example, some with lung cancer find it easier to breath right before dying, as if they were cured before leaving Earth. I can't help being amazed by

God's awesome presence during this time in life. So, similar to the human life cycle, the objects in this grove are
serving their retirement before the final end of their life
cycle. I never fathomed finding the sacred in my parents'
grove. However, after reflecting on this space, I realized
that I am surrounded by sacred symbols in this grove.

As our students grew from thinking about religious spaces
to thinking about how the sacred appears in the visual in ordinary spaces, they started to have some remarkable insights about
the way the sacred appears in all areas of their lives. One student
(call her "Susan") reflected on the spaces we inhabit, looking
at them through the twin lenses of Joan Chittister's "Monastic
Wisdom for Seekers of Light"[18] and Stephen Nachmanovitch's
"Free Play: Improvisation in Life and Art:"[19] "I thought the article
by Nachmanovitch really coincided with Chittister's—getting
across the idea that this sterilized world of destruction is sorely
in need of beauty and creativeness for the sake of our souls. "Not
art for art's sake, but art for life's sake" (Nachmanovitch). We can't
right all the problems in the world, but we can make our little
section of it beautiful, whether physically or simply with beautiful character."

Since they had to make postings on our class website quite
frequently, our students quickly got over any concerns about let-
ting others see and comment on their work and began to develop a supportive community of commentary on one another's
insights. Another student, a physics and math major, commented
on Susan's posting, saying:

> I quite agree with this. Now just think if everyone would
> make a small contribution. I mean 6.5 billion contribu-
> tions no matter how small would amount to an unimagi-
> nable total. Now I don't mean that everyone must paint
> a Rembrandt or anything like that. All it would take is

18. Chittister's piece is the last chapter of Thiessen's *Theological Aesthetics*.

19. Stephen Nachmanovitch, *Free Play: Improvisation in Life and Art* (New
York: Tarcher, 1991).

> someone picking up a piece of trash off the ground or
> maybe just a smile instead of a blank stare. If everyone
> chipped in the world would be far better. Life on this
> earth has been caught up in our drole daily routines, and
> nobody pays much attention anymore to the little things
> that help make life more fulfilling. It's these little things
> that I think Nachmanovitch was referring to. Again
> not specific art pieces but art in a more general sense.
> Preserving beauty and enhancing it. In a sense recreating
> as well.

These students were not trained as theologians nor as artists; but each of them wound up showing both interest in the visual and the sacred, and fairly profound sensitivity and insight.

Image of the Day

Our Image of the Day project begins as an exercise in seeing, and even more importantly it becomes a way of deliberately seeking out meaning in one's life and the images one sees everyday. Four times a week, each student is required to post on a forum in our class website an image of an exceptional encounter in their day, and to comment on four other postings. The image of the day idea originally grew out of a History of Media class taught by Alex Sweetman at the University of Colorado at Boulder in the 1990s. The idea is to pay attention to when the stage curtains lift on your everyday experience and you witness something remark-able that takes you out of the ordinary into the extraordinary. Our students can use photography or any other medium to con-vey their image of the day, and the project is left fairly vague and open-ended. The image can be something seen, or it could come from a dream, or result from a conversation, for example. When they post their images, students must accompany the image with some text ascribing the meaning the image held for the student.

It turns out that meaning itself is quite difficult to locate in the visual. Students initially preferred to posture their comments in criticism to what they saw rather than to replay each day's events and seek out something that revealed itself in an extraordinary and meaningful way. As we insist on only images which contain meaning, students must constantly strip the packaging of reception to locate the images which matter most to each of them. The accumulated series of images records a kind of map over which a pattern of seeing begins to reveal itself. As the semester closes, students can identify this pattern and stage in life as they assess what has been of value and meaning to them at the end of their undergraduate school experience.

One real benefit of this project comes through the additional requirement that students view the postings of their classmates and post comments about them. The result is that the students become a *community* of observers, not merely an agglomeration of individual observers. While they can at times be critical of one another, this is almost always helpful, and they very frequently enter into the wonder of the moment with one another. It is worth recalling Aristotle's comment that the love of wisdom begins with wonder; it is equally worth recalling that the root of the word "miracle" is a Latin word meaning "to wonder." Over the course of the semester, we required the students to make roughly one hundred and fifty postings each to our class website, including their own work and their responses to others' work. When we first announced this in class, the students were concerned it would be too heavy a load. By the end of the semester, we estimate that together they had made a thousand more postings than were required. We suspect that our students were able to make the move from thinking of the assignments as work to thinking of them as opportunity to have substantial conversations and to make significant pieces of art in a supportive community. It does not surprise us to learn that they were hungry for both of these things. Often the discussions online led to what we identified were the most salient topics for the following week's in-class discussion.

The Sacred Line Project

A third project builds on the reflective exercise in seeing and wondering from the Image of the Day exercise. The Sacred Line Project simply asks students to recall the most sacred line they walk in any given week, and then to make that line visible, literally, in the environment. We purposefully ask our students to seek out the sacred in their everyday life. As with the Site Visits, we do not give them any more guidance than that—the assignment is left intentionally open—and we steadfastly refuse to define what the sacred is. This requires the students to first define the sacred for themselves and then reflect on where that occurs in their everyday life.

As instructors, it has been revealing to us that no one has ever pleaded an absence of the sacred in their daily life and opted out of this assignment. All our students have been able to locate the sacred in their weekly walk of life. Once again, some of them do balk at the openness and perceived lack of definition of the assignment. Some have asked us to define what a line is, how to mark a line, and what our definition of the sacred is. We reply to them that if the words are meaningful enough that they can use them, then what do they point to in their ordinary experience? Part meditation, part direct engagement in temporary public art installation, our aim is to help the students to examine their own daily practices to see which of them most correspond to the sacred; then to do something to demarcate that line visually.

The second part of this assignment, requiring students to physically mark their environment to indicate their sacred line, was a way for us to ask students to intentionally engage with real materials in a physical act to mark a place (without mentioning that they were creating site-specific temporary public artworks). Students can place, create, remove, transform, relocate, or in some way do something physical to mark their line and to make it visible to us and others. How students did this, their process, what materials they chose, their permanency, context, and any relationship to traditional liturgical materials, natural processes,

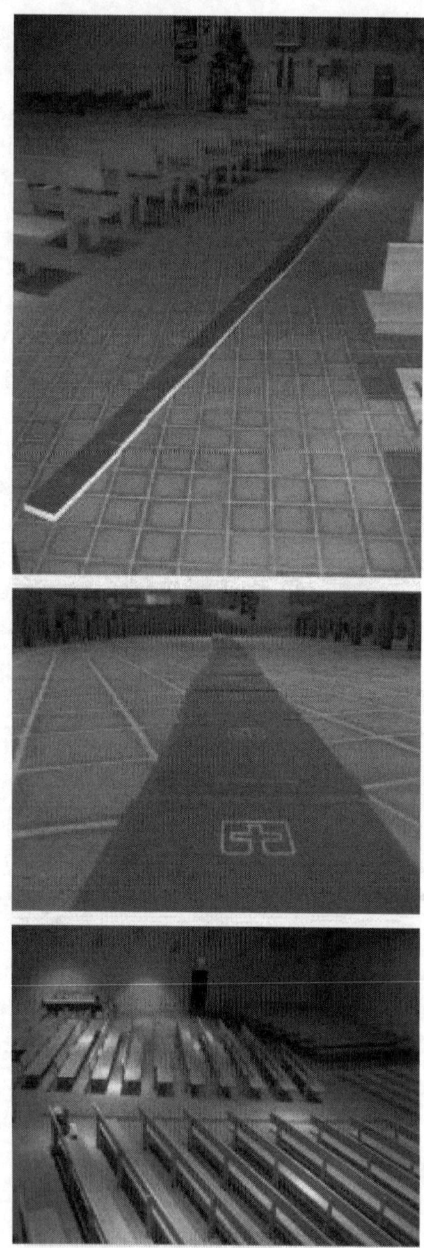

FIGURE 4: Frank Johnson, *Sacred Line*

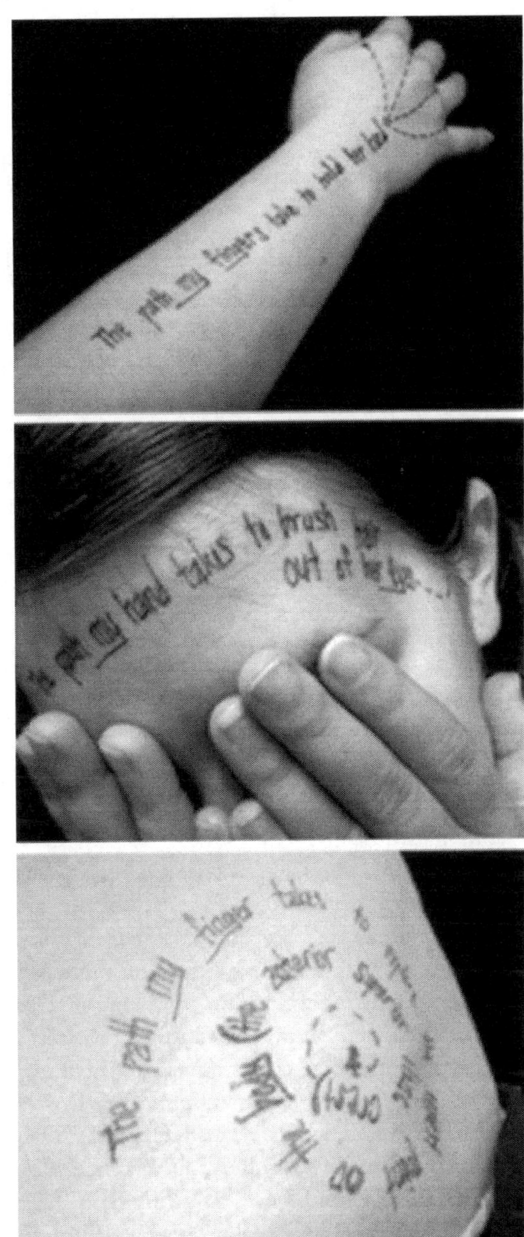

FIGURE 5: Kiel Mutschelknaus, *Sacred Line*

135

etc. become critical elements for discussing how effectively they conveyed the sacredness of their walk.

For one student, Frank Johnson, his sacred line was in a traditional sacred space and marked by the books that were his connection to an historical and present community. (Frank is now a seminarian at Luther Seminary.) For Kiel Mutschelknaus, the sacred was in another kind of sacred space altogether, on the body of his lover.

Another student, whom we will call "Allie," marked the snow in front of the courthouse with rose petals and then photographed the scene from several angles. She wrote:

> Every Tuesday morning for the past two months or so I have walked this same path without giving much thought to its sanctity. It's not a walk I much enjoy, but one I realize I desperately need. It is a walk of service, and hopefully it is a walk of love. For an hour or two a week I travel to the courthouse to serve as an advocate in the courtroom for the Rape and Domestic Abuse Center. I listen to protection order cases dealing with either domestic abuse, rape, or stalking charges. It's not an easy path to stay on each week, sometimes I leave in tears, yet this walk has nothing to do with me or my comfortability, so I go. I have come to believe that my life without service to others is one I am not willing to live.
>
> This wise man once said to love the lord your God and to love your neighbors as yourself. The wife at the stand, testifying against her husband's violence, is my neighbor; so is the husband. I am here on this earth to serve and love them both. I know that kind of service and love can happen anywhere, but this is the walk that I know I can point to as sacred because I would not be walking it if it weren't for Christ.
>
> I marked the snow next to the sidewalk with rose petals. They are in no way in the shape of a line because there is no progress to be made on this walk. The part of me that selfishly wants to block out the pain of others always stays outside that building defiantly, while the part of me that desperately cries out to God for the

anguish of His people never goes home. I encircled the petals with a heart and wrote in the snow, "To those who suffer injustice."

Allie's sacred line is one that is full of pain. The rose petals on the snow seemed to call the mind's eye rapidly back and forth between the beauty of the roses and the suggestion of a trail of blood. It was a simple gesture but one that took courage to enact, and that bespoke even deeper courage in Allie.

Other students considered both the lines they walked and the ways in which they walked them. After this exercise, for weeks afterwards our students were discovering the signs of sacred lines other students had left on the landscape, most notably small stones marked with a white painted cross and left all along one student's path. This may seem trivial, but the effect was to mark our whole campus and parts of town off-campus as well, with traces of the sacred.

One-Minute Video

The One-Minute Video project is an attempt to evoke the transcendent in the ordinary. Students create, edit, produce and present a one-minute experimental video. The movie must unfold in a progression of events that employs some notion of transcendence, redemption, and being. The rules are simple: no slide shows, and all audio tracks must be built from diegetic sound. The sixty seconds can utilize hand-drawn animation, claymation, stop-motion photography, vector-tweens, compositing in After Effects, etc. Students must also play with the standard 24 frames of video allotted to a second of real time: resulting in videos that were either slowed-down, sped up, played backwards, etc., or made use of stop-motion photography or hand-drawn animation without reference to a video camera at all.

Perhaps the most profound video project was one by Nicole Harrison. Nicole's video recalled the work of Ana Mendieta's early performance art in nearby Iowa. While playing the Led Zeppelin

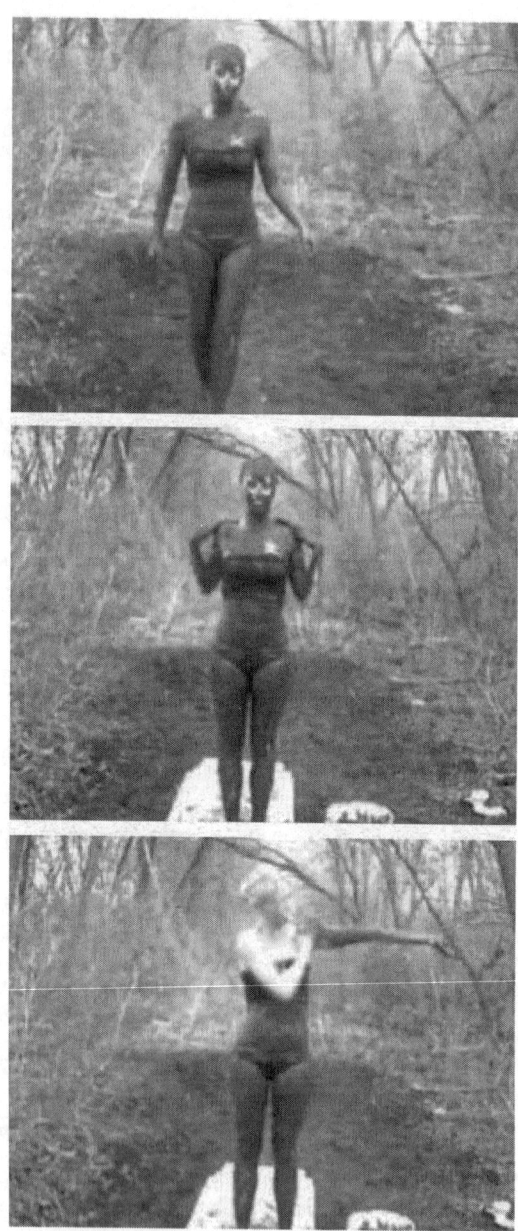

FIGURE 6: Nicole Harrison, *One-Minute Video*

classic "Stairway to Heaven," we see the video unfold in an unnerving backwards sequence. She, a woman who is completely covered in mud and almost indiscernible, rises from the ground. Once standing, she reaches from the earth to wipe her body, first her face, then one arm, and then the other, followed by her torso and legs. She finishes by writing "The End" in mud and laughs. This courageous reference to a bodily resurrection was made all the more vivid to the class who knew that this student's sister and another friend had recently died in an auto accident.

CONCLUSION

This class is a work in progress, and we hope our presentation of it here has not come across as a dogmatic how-to piece. If anything, we are trying to model for our students what we tried to teach them, namely, that it matters immensely that we continue to reflect on the relation between visual culture and the sacred. As we look back on it and refine it, a few elements strike us as especially worth preserving: openness, a willingness to play with new media, an atmosphere of respect and of wonder. Openness and open-endedness in the assignments are challenging for students accustomed to specific assignments, but we think the challenge is a good one, one that can lead to exploration of how the sacred can emerge in the profane. Playfulness, when done with respect for others, invites a return to wonder and awe, which are so often discouraged in education when, in fact, they might be key to real learning, as Schiller suggested.[20]

Honesty demands that we point out that not all our students liked this class. What is interesting is that no one has objected to our use of art, and, despite a relatively broad set of religious backgrounds, none of them object to the class on religious grounds. Those who voiced dislike for the class found it too open-ended.

---

20. We are thinking of his *On the Aesthetic Education of Man,* and especially passages like the fifteenth letter, where he says that play is what makes us complete, and that we don't play for utility's sake so much as for the sake of beauty.

Since we do not intend to indoctrinate them so much as to invite them to explore, we admit that we have no remedy for that objection. Its open-endedness has certainly enabled us teachers to learn from one another, and we hope that it has also made it more possible for our students to continue to grow as both learners and as doers well after the class has ended.

It's too early to know what the full effects of this class will be, but we think we have caught enough glimpses of some powerful moments to believe that it will make some difference in the ways our students regard both the visual and the sacred. We have no pretensions of being able to produce mystics by showing them chancels. But we are pleased with the ways in which our students begin to see, if not the chancels, then the historical perspective of those chancels that have both represented and enclosed the sacred for them. In order to think of one's place of work and life as hallowed ground, it is simply not enough to work at a church-related college. The steeples of the prairie draw one's eye and send it skyward at the same time, simultaneously attracting and deflecting the gaze that seeks the sacred. But when students line the floor with books, paint themselves with the soil they walk on, trace the sacred lines their feet and hands daily seek, and do so in wondering mutual community, one wonders if one isn't seeing a new generation of potential mystics sitting in the chairs in one's classroom.

Contributors

RONALD R. BERNIER is an assistant professor in the Department of Humanities, Social Sciences, and Management at Wentworth Institute of Technology in Boston, Massachusetts.

JASON A. DANNER, doctoral candidate in the Department of Religious Studies at the University of Virginia, has taught at the College of William and Mary in Williamsburg, Virginia, and currently resides in Kyoto, Japan.

KAREN GONZÁLEZ RICE is a doctoral candidate and teaches in the Department of Art, Art History, and Visual Studies at Duke University.

MICHELLE LANG, independent scholar, was formerly an assistant professor of art history at the University of Nebraska–Kearney.

SCOTT PARSONS is an assistant professor of art and anthropology at Augustana College in Sioux Falls, South Dakota.

ARTHUR PONTYNEN is a professor of art history at the University of Wisconsin–Oshkosh

DAVID O'HARA is an assistant professor of philosophy and classics at Augustana College in Sioux Falls, South Dakota.

DANIEL A. SIEDELL is an assistant professor of modern and contemporary art, art history, theory, and criticism at the University of Nebraska–Omaha.